Alternatives to Women's Imprisonment

Alternatives to Women's Imprisonment

Pat Carlen

Open University Press
Milton Keynes • Philadelphia

Open University Press
Celtic Court
22 Ballmoor
Buckingham
MK18 1XW

and
1900 Frost Road, Suite 101
Bristol, PA 19007, USA

First Published 1990

British Library Cataloguing in Publication Data
Carlen, Pat
  Alternatives to women's imprisonment.
  1. Great Britain. Penal System. Reform
  I. Title
  365'.7'0941

  ISBN 0 335 09926 2
       0 335 09925 4 (pbk)

Library of Congress Cataloging-in-Publication Data
Carlen, Pat.
    Alternatives to women's imprisonment/by Pat Carlen.
      p. cm.
    Includes bibliographical references.
    ISBN 0–335–09926–2. ISBN 0–335–09925–4 (pbk.)
    1. Women prisoners–England. 2. Women prisoners–Wales.
  3. Female offenders–Services for–England. 4. Female offenders–
  –Services for–Wales. I. Title.
  HV9649.E5C37 1990
  364.3'74'0942–dc20   89–48788 CIP

Typeset by Inforum Typesetting, Portsmouth
Printed in Great Britain by St Edmundsbury Press Ltd,
Bury St Edmunds, Suffolk

Alternatives to Women's Imprisonment
is dedicated to the campaigning and self-help
ex-prisoner-run organizations

Women in Prison
Clean Break
Creative and Supportive Trust (CAST)

Contents

Acknowledgements

Several institutions and many individuals contributed to the research reported in the following pages. Pre-eminently I am grateful to: the Nuffield Foundation, for funding the project with a small grant of £1,110; the University of Keele, for allowing me a term's paid leave of absence to visit the hostels, the projects and the prisons; the Association of Chief Probation Officers, for granting me permission to approach individual probation services for help with the research; the Inner London, Greater Manchester, West Midlands and Staffordshire Probation Services for giving me detailed assistance; the probation services listed in the Appendix for completing the questionnaire on non-custodial projects for women; the staff of the non-custodial projects and hostels listed in the Appendix for making time to speak to me; the staff at the prisons listed in the Appendix who gave me either oral or written information.

In particular, I thank the following individuals: Lydia Arnold, Glasmin Banton-Douglas, Eleanor Barry, Christine Braddock, Fran Brody, Gill Brown, Rosemary Brown, Daniel Carlen, Jill Carlen, Peter Carlen, J. Chadwick, Jan Clare, R. Clayton, Ms Cocker (Askham Grange), Debbie Coles, Mr Crouch (Drake Hall), M. Day, R.G. Franklin, Sue Fricker, Mike Gander, Elaine Guest, Ros Hamilton, Jean Hankinson, John Harris, R. Harris, Jenny Hicks, Moira Honnan, Fiona Hope, Marie Hurley, Michael Johnson, Valentina Kindjarsey, Mike Kosh, Phil Lloyd, Sandy Lydon, Doris MacDonald, Tracy McClure, Kaff McClusky, Helen McFarlane, Rosy Meehan, J. Mood, Hilary Newman, Angela Noonan, Josie O'Dwyer, Sheila Pallister, Anna Parava, Alastair Peacock, June Peters, Henry Pickering, Sue Priest, Stephen Prior, Lesley Pym, Lorna Reid, S. Redshaw, S. Robotham, Jean Ross, David Seary, Laurence Singer, Sheila Shufflebottom, R. Smith, Stephen Stanley, Joy Stanyer, Lesley Steele, Aysha Tarzi, Chris Tchaikovsky, Nicky Vassall, Robert Verity, Del White, Judi Wilson and Cliff Young.

For help with my researches in California I thank: Ellen Barry, Robert Cancilla, Naneen Karraker, Teri Kolze, Louise Minnick, Glenda Parmentier and Phyllis Walker. For telling me so much about Australian prisons, I thank David Brown and Hilary Kramer.

For kindly granting permission to reprint extracts from works on which they hold copyright, I acknowledge: the Creative and Supportive Trust (CAST) and Jeanine Cresswell for permission to reproduce an extract from the CAST 1986–7 Report; Clean Break and Jacki Holborough and Gilli Mebarek for permission to reproduce extracts from the Clean Break 1986–7 Report; the North London Education Project for permission to reproduce extracts from their 1986 Report; the Central London Social Security Advisers Forum (CLSSAF) for permission to reproduce three extracts from *True Horror Stories*, 1989.

Finally, I acknowledge with gratitude: Stanford University's Institute for Research on Women and Gender for an Exxon Summer Fellowship which allowed me to study women's jails in California during July and August 1987; the Australian Institute of Criminology whose invitation to deliver a paper at their 1987 Seminar in Tasmania on 'Crime in the Future' spurred me to develop some of the ideas on women and crime in the future which are reproduced in Chapter 1; Stephen Shaw, Director of the Prison Reform Trust whose 1989 invitation to give a public lecture entitled 'Women's Imprisonment: A Strategy for Abolition' forced me to confront the issues of reductionism and abolition considered in Chapter 5; and John Skelton of Open University Press for support and patience.

Doreen Thompson typed the whole manuscript quickly and efficiently and I am grateful to her for that – and much else besides.

Pat Carlen
University of Keele, Centre for Criminology

Tables

Statutes

Abbreviations

ACOP	Association of Chief Officers of Probation
ACPO	Assistant Chief Probation Officer
ARP	Alcohol Recovery Project
CAB	Citizens' Advice Bureau
CAS	Co-ordinated Accommodation Scheme
CAST	Creative and Supportive Trust
CPAG	Child Poverty Action Group
CS	Community Service
CSO	Community Service Order
DHSS	Department of Health and Social Security (now DSS)
DSS	Department of Social Security
MADD	Mothers Against Drinking and Driving
SPO	Senior Probation Officer
WIP	Women in Prison
WPRC	Women Prisoners' Resource Centre

Introduction

Women have served all these centuries as looking glasses possessing the magic and delicious power of reflecting the figure of man at twice its natural size.

(Virginia Woolf, *A Room of One's Own*, first published 1929, in Woolf, 1963:37)

Feminist literature abundantly testifies to the profound sense of underachievement scarring the lives of many women. Traditionally isolated from the most important arenas of public life, women have usually not been compensated for such segregation by finding emotional fulfilment and a proper valuation of their talents within the domestic sphere. 'It feels sad to be a woman,' wrote Vera Brittain in 1913. 'Men seem to have so much more choice as to what they are intended for' (Brittain, 1979:59), and these sentiments are still echoed by untold numbers of women whose lives have been stunted by gender conventions and in the service of men. For it has not only been middle-class women who have felt stifled by the trammels of a gender oppression that denies them the space to develop socially, emotionally and intellectually. The poverty, poor housing, unemployment and long hours of domestic labour of many working-class women are to this day frequently aggravated by their loneliness, isolation and a despairing sense of futility. Certainly women in prison have again and again told me that as teenagers they were denied the freedom and opportunities for development allowed to their brothers (McRobbie and Garber, 1976; Christina and Carlen, 1985), and that upon marriage they were discouraged from having non-family friends (cf. Hunt, 1983; Carlen, 1983a, 1988). Lone mothers, lesbians and young women on the run from local authority Care can experience an even greater isolation. Once they break the law it is the misfortune of isolated or otherwise unconventional women that they are more likely to receive a custodial penalty for a relatively minor crime than are men or women with families (Worrall, 1981; Carlen, 1983a, Farrington and Morris, 1983a, 1983b). Sentenced to imprisonment, already isolated or depressed women are too often launched on a downward spiral. For them (and many others)

Prison is not only damaging during the course of a sentence. Coming out has its own problems, and the snowballing effects of imprisonment are felt long after release . . . many women will have entered prison as a direct result of being homeless and unsupported. Others will have had drink and drug-related problems together with mental and emotional difficulties. A majority will have had histories of institutionalisation. When they leave prison their prospects of survival are disgustingly dim [because] the limited resources and support available for women leaving prison actually cater for very few.

(O'Dwyer *et al.*, 1987)

Upon their release from custody, many women will claim that the *only* good thing about prison was that it engendered in them a greater appreciation of women's worth and capabilities, as well as a realization that at least some of their problems may have stemmed from too great a dependency upon men (cf. Hicks and Carlen, 1985). In view, therefore, of the vast feminist literature on the need for women to circumvent the demands of traditional gender controls and develop as strong persons in their own right, in view, too, of our increasing knowledge of the particular needs of women law-breakers and ex-prisoners (O'Dwyer *et al.*, 1987), there has been an astonishing dearth of supportive and rehabilitative programmes fashioned specifically for female offenders. It was in order to investigate the extent to which women's special needs had been put on the agendas of probation and other agencies providing for offenders and ex-prisoners that in 1988 I undertook a small empirical investigation entitled 'Alternatives to Women's Imprisonment'.

The investigation

Although many research and official reports have suggested that it is unnecessary for even 3 per cent of the prison population to be composed of women, more women are being sent to prison each year. Moreover, despite the fact that 'alternatives to women's imprisonment' are continually and ritualistically invoked and prescribed, very little is known about existing provision for women offenders and ex-prisoners, while even less is known about the successful projects and housing schemes which *do* offer alternative life-styles to previously institutionalized and/or transient women and young girls. This is not surprising. For what *is* an alternative to imprisonment? Can 'alternatives to imprisonment' be conceptualized independently of the continuing debates about 'reductionism' and 'abolition' (Mathiesen, 1974; Bianchi and Swaaningen, 1986)? And if they can, is it desirable that they *should* be? More specifically to our topic here: to what extent can analysis of the 'alternatives to women's imprisonment' illuminate reductionist and abolitionist issues relating to the whole prison population? All of these questions will be addressed in this book, which owes its existence to a Nuffield sponsored empirical study of 'alternatives to women's imprisonment' conducted in 1988.

As originally conceived, the 1988 study set out to:

1 Investigate, analyse and compare inter-agency co-operation in the provision of

non-custodial facilities for women in Manchester, Birmingham and Stoke-on-Trent.

2 Investigate, analyse and compare inter-agency co-operation in the provision of non-custodial facilities for convicted women and after-care facilities for women ex-prisoners in Manchester, Birmingham and Stoke-on-Trent.

3 Describe and analyse the work of some of the new projects for female offenders and ex-prisoners.

4 Suggest ways in which new alternatives to women's imprisonment might halt the 'revolving door syndrome' and help convicted women and ex-prisoners rebuild their lives without falling foul of the law again.

The major investigative methods planned were:

1 A postal questionnaire to all probation services in England, Wales and Northern Ireland to assess the range of provision specifically for women and to locate new projects.

2 Visits to all women's groups and hostels in Birmingham, Stoke and Manchester to gain information via focused interviews with staff.

3 Theoretical analysis of the empirical data using constructs from modern criminological theory and inter-agency analyses (as in Carlen, 1983a and 1976).

But the study was not carried out exactly as originally conceived for several (often interrelated) reasons: some stemming from failures of theoretical and practical planning on my part; others inherent in qualitative research, the aims and methods of which must necessarily be more open to constant reconceptualization than those of quantitative investigations; most related to the very nature of the subject in question.

The fundamental error on my part at the beginning of this research was a failure to equip myself with working definitions of 'provision for women' and 'alternatives to imprisonment'. Representatives of three probation services did contact me for clarification concerning 'provision for women', and they and all other respondents appeared ultimately to interpret my questions as referring to programmes and hostels *specifically* for women offenders, often indicating, too, the special conditions affecting the extent of provision for women by their services. (These usually referred either to the very small number of women given custodial sentences in their particular areas and/or to the financial constraints experienced by relatively small probation services.) In part, the failure to define 'provision for women' and 'alternatives' was deliberate – I had wanted to find out how probation officers themselves defined them. However, I should have known better than to attempt an exploration in semantics via a postal questionnaire, and these initial failures of definition resulted in my being unable to use the returned questionnaires for comparative purposes, and may also have affected the response rate – which was only 70 per cent.

The failure to define 'alternatives' narrowly was more deliberate (and, in the end, more productive) than the failure to define 'provision for women'. For the questionnaire instructions did at least distinguish between two definitions of 'alternatives'. The first referred specifically to non-custodial alternatives acceptable to sentencers at times when the seriousness of the offence would, in the absence of an acceptable alternative, have resulted in a prison or youth custody sentence:

> I would be grateful if you would list below the names and addresses of local residential (e.g. hostel) or non-residential programmes or facilities for women offenders that in your opinion are acceptable to sentencers as being credible alternatives to custodial sentences.

The second allowed for a wider interpretation and referred more to rehabilitation and prevention than to the narrowly conceived 'alternatives' to tariff sentencing where it is increasingly assumed that a 'non-custodial alternative' is only acceptable to sentencers if it strives to bring the transcarceral pains of imprisonment into the community (see Home Office, 1988c). The second instruction, therefore, was:

> I would be grateful if you would list below any local programmes known to you that provide women with a type of support aimed at keeping them out of prison (or trouble) in future (e.g. probation programmes specifically designed for women offenders, befriending schemes, etc.).

Yet, even with this degree of definition the very nature of the topic in question resulted in many respondents listing all the relevant projects and hostels under the first instruction with one or more of the following explanations appended. First, even when sentencers *are* provided with what should be acceptable alternatives to custody, they too often use them merely as alternatives to each other and thereby subvert the whole concept of alternatives (cf. Featherstone, 1987:8). Second, their own professional judgements about what should be seen as acceptable alternatives to custody were so different to the more punitive expectations of magistrates and judges that they found it difficult to claim that specific projects *were* acceptable to sentencers, even though, in the respondents' opinions, the ones they listed should have been. Third, though they believed that 'officially' the only acceptable non-custodial alternative (apart from a Community Service Order) was thought to be a day centre attendance order made under Schedule 11 section 4(B) of the 1982 Criminal Justice Act, they themselves felt that other, less formal probation provision should also be acceptable, and had therefore included such provision in their returned questionnaires. Mair explains the distinction between Schedule 11 section 4(B) day centres and the rest:

> Schedule 11 section 4(B) of the 1982 Criminal Justice Act provided that during a probation order an offender could be required to attend at a day centre for a period of up to 60 days; and such centres had to be approved by the local probation committee. Thus, since the Act, there have been two kinds of day centre (which may not be easily separable in practice): the more

informal, and voluntary kind which tends to cater for inadequates whether they are offenders or not; and the 4(B) kind which is generally seen as providing a 'heavy end' alternative to custody, and whose [sic] most enthusiastic supporters tend to see as the only viable alternative to a custodial sentence.

(Mair, 1988:2)

As it turned out, discussion as to what *is* an alternative to imprisonment and whether 'alternative' should be defined narrowly as a programme rigorous enough either to satisfy sentencers' punitive intentions or to match up with their (often mistaken) beliefs about what will deter people from future law-breaking, became central to most interviews with prison and criminal justice personnel, and is now a central theme of this book. However, once I myself decided that 'alternatives' to imprisonment should include any programme of intervention likely to deter someone from future criminal activity, it also seemed appropriate to investigate rehabilitative programmes currently operative in the women's penal institutions. Ironical in a project entitled 'Alternatives to Women's Imprisonment'? Yes, but in order to 'place' the project within a theorization of reductionism and abolition, it also seemed desirable to assess any positively rehabilitative (i.e. self-destruct) programmes that the women's gaols and youth custody centres might be providing.

Another 'alternative' that had to be touched on was the Community Service Order (CSO). Although I had originally decided that because at least something was known about Community Service Orders for women (see Dominelli, 1984; Mitra, 1983, quoted in Walker, 1985:69) I myself should concentrate on accommodation and supportive groups and exclude CSOs from the study, the problems (either real or assumed) of community service for women surfaced in so many discussions with probation officers that I gratefully accepted an invitation from the organizers of Community Service in Hanley (Staffordshire) to get some first-hand views on how the system was working for women there.

The very nature of rehabilitative provision for women was the major reason for the empirical study not turning out as planned. Because many programmes and projects for women are dependent upon voluntary and short-term support, they are also often relatively unknown in the early stages of their work and then forced by lack of finance to close down just as the statutory agencies are getting to know about them. Likewise (and as will be discussed in Chapter 4) many probation-run women's groups exist only while there are officers in post interested in running them. For these reasons I was not able to make a rigorous comparison of the range of rehabilitative provision available for women offenders in Birmingham, Manchester and Stoke, even though I had tremendous help from the probation services of all three areas. At the same time, and as a result of the relative scarcity of provision for the comparatively few female offenders and women ex-prisoners, in all three geographical areas originally chosen for comparison reference was constantly made to services available (and used by my respondents) outside the area in question. This was particularly so for hostels and other services provided in inner

London. I therefore visited several projects and hostels in Central, North and South London with the especial aims of talking to: (a) the organizers of non-statutory bodies like CAST (Creative and Supportive Trust – for women only), WIP (Women in Prison) and Clean Break (the women ex-prisoners' theatre company); (b) the wardens of hostels with policies of taking some of the most difficult-to-place women; and (c) the organizers of distinctive projects such as the North London Education Project and the Women's Motor Mechanics Workshop Ltd. As the project proceeded I spoke to more and more people about their work with women offenders and, as recurring themes began to emerge, I was able to compare some of the issues arising with those that had been current in those women's jails and prisons of California (USA), Tasmania and Melbourne (Australia) which I had had the opportunity to visit in 1987.

So, that is what I did. This book is what was made of it.

The book's rationale, 'structure and arguments'

Rationale

Despite the plethora of publications which in the last ten years has borne witness to the waste of women's imprisonment and the inappropriateness of penal custody as a punishment for all but a tiny minority of female offenders, little has been said about the alternatives to women's imprisonment, or about why imprisonment continues to exist and, in the absence of countermeasures, is likely to enmesh even more women in the future. Partly, this has been a consequence of 'alternatives to imprisonment' always being interpreted as referring to *sentencing* alternatives and the concomitant awareness of campaigners that although a range of appropriate non-custodial sentencing alternatives is already available, sentencers tend to use them as alternatives to each other rather than as alternatives to imprisonment. Partly, it has followed from the reluctance of some of the more radical anti-imprisonment writers and campaigners to engage in discussion of alternatives to prison, fearing that positive reforms in the short-term can frequently have a corrupting effect on the more desirable long-term goal of abolition (Mathiesen, 1974:210). And partly it has stemmed from a libertarian and anti-materialist reluctance to recognize that a majority of women going to prison *do* have problems which, though not best dealt with by the criminal justice or penal systems, call for some type of intervention – usually in the name of social justice and often, too, in the cause of future crime prevention.

The research on which this book is based was conceived not so much with the idea of examining sentencing practice, but more with the aims of investigating (1) the positive aspects (if any) of prison regimes which might reduce the likelihood of a woman either re-offending or being returned to gaol; and (2) the actual non-custodial provision available for those deemed by the courts as suitable for a non-custodial sentence. This approach, in turn, was taken because of (1) knowledge that imprisonment occurs often for reasons quite unconnected with criminal justice, e.g. because of 'community care' policies of regional health authorities reluctant to hospitalize 'difficult' patients likely to be in need of residential care for indefinite periods of time, or because a woman has no fixed address and/or the relevant agencies are thoroughly fed up with her recidivism and/or addiction; (2) awareness of the existence of a number of very successful projects and hostels, knowledge of which should be spread in order to underline the female anti-imprisonment lobby's message that there *are* alternatives to women's imprisonment; and (3) a theoretical and political commitment to analysing all aspects of criminal justice within a consideration of government policies relating to social justice in general (see Carlen, 1980, 1983b, 1988, and 1989). This approach displaces crime and punishment from their conventional disciplines of criminology and penology and conceives their contemporary forms as being irremediably related to the conditions in which recent government legislation on welfare, housing, local government, education, privatization, etc. has been realized. (See Gamble and Wells, 1989 for good analyses of 'Thatcher's Law' as it has affected education, housing, criminal justice, privatization and welfare.)

Structure and arguments

The main arguments of the book are presented here because they also inform the analyses and are in part responsible for the book's structure, a structure which constantly has to switch back and forth between ethnographic analysis of the existing alternatives to women's imprisonment and description of the economic, political and ideological conditions which subvert them.

1 Chapter 1 briefly summarizes current trends in women's crimes and women's imprisonment.
2 In Chapter 2 it is argued that although a number of education and pre-release initiatives presently being developed in the women's prisons aim to undo the harm that prison does, other aspects of the penal regimes undermine the rehabilitative schemes to such an extent that in most cases imprisonment for women cannot be justified as part of a comprehensive crime reduction programme.
3 Chapter 3 describes the range of accommodation available to homeless women in trouble and contends that although the knowledge and expertise for designing and administering a comprehensive housing programme for them already exists, its effective implementation is obstructed by government policies aimed at regulating the economy via the development of a strong central state and by sexist ideologies concerning the governance of adolescent young women, motherhood and the family.
4 Chapter 4 describes a variety of probation-run and ex-prisoner self-help projects and argues (1) that although the Government continues to pay lip-service to the

notion that a reduction in the prison population is desirable, the adverse effects
of its own punitive transcarceral policies (see 7 below), as evidenced in the 1988
Green Paper, *Punishment, Custody and the Community*, make such a reduction
unlikely; and (2) that the good work of all such programmes is repeatedly
atrophied by lack of adequate funding and by housing and employment ideologies and practices which discriminate against women in trouble and black
women in trouble in particular.

5 The economic conditions in which abortive attempts have been made to reduce
the numbers of men and women going to prison in the 1980s have been shaped
by a government which 'took office with a self-consciously radical strategy
involving a "rolling back of the state", the dismantling of corporatist forms and
the implementation of liberal free-market policies aiming to reverse economic
decline' (Graham and Prosser, 1988). The monetarist rhetoric which demanded
a reduction in public expenditure also called for a weakening of local government and a strengthening of the central state. So, although, as Stuart Hall and
Martin Jacques (1983:12) write, 'it is difficult to call an economic strategy which
results in some four million unemployed and the shutting down of substantial
sectors of the economy, a success', the political ramifications of the strategy have
severely limited the extent to which the local state can nowadays ameliorate the
suffering of homeless and destitute people who, more often than not, are themselves the sacrificial victims of central government economic policies. Moreover, the striking increases in wealth and income inequalities which have been a
feature of the last decade (Byrne, 1987) have fallen most heavily upon women,
over one million of whom head one-parent families and for whom unemployment has increased more rapidly than it has for men (Bull and Wilding,
1983:22). Government determination to minimalize the role of state welfare
provoked cuts in benefits under the 1986 Social Security Act and the Housing
Act 1988 which have aggravated women's poverty still further.

6 The political changes of the last ten years have also had a direct effect on the
development of local non-custodial alternatives. Reducing the powers of local
councils has resulted in them being unable to respond adequately to specific
local needs, while the abolition of the Greater London Council by the 1985
Local Government Act had adverse effects on the work of some voluntary
groups when their funding was temporarily put in jeopardy and, in some cases,
reduced. Furthermore, the 1988 Local Government Act with its clause prohibit-
ing the intentional promotion of homosexuality may inhibit the development of
schemes designed to help lesbians counter discrimination in housing.

7 Ideologically, women's imprisonment is currently affected by three major facets of
government policies. First, by the renewed emphasis on women's place in the
family which has transferred the burdens of caring for the young and incapacitated
from the reduced budgets of welfare and health authorities onto the shoulders of
mothers, wives, daughters and other female family members. Second, by 'the
Government's philosophy of crime reduction [which] has encouraged the idea

that prison is a deterrence against crime' (Wiles, 1988:166) and which has resulted in more women going to prison for longer periods. Third, by the Government's more recent need to reduce the prison population and thereby halt the ever-expanding prison-building programme which by mid-1988 had cost almost £1 billion (Home Office, 1988c). Yet this last turnabout in government penal strategy has been accompanied by only a slight diminution of punitive rhetoric. According to *Punishment, Custody and the Community* (Home Office, 1988c) the pains of imprisonment are still to be imposed, but they are to be fashioned more cheaply in the community and via a tightening up of the non-custodial alternatives. For backup, of course, these stiffer non-custodials will be reinforced by the other transcarceral measures already taken by the Thatcher Governments, e.g. the 1984 Trade Union Act with its punitive clauses imposing restrictions on trade union activities and expenditure, a decade of punitive legislation directed against high-spending local authorities (see Leach and Stoker, 1988), and increasingly punitive social security and employment legislation designed to serve 'the economic needs of a wage-labour market' (Alcock, 1989:105). One problem for the Government's plans for community punishments is that because punitive crime policies are directed almost exclusively at the already disadvantaged, many petty offenders will be unable to take any more punishment in the community. They will fail, therefore, to complete a non-custodial order, and end up in gaol anyhow (see Carlen, 1989 on the non-feasibility of extremely punitive non-custodial schemes).

8 The major conclusion drawn from the research reported here is that although some excellent non-custodial rehabilitative schemes for women offenders already exist, they are by and large rendered ineffective in reducing women's imprisonment: first, because they are too few and far between; and second, because government legislation in other spheres systematically subverts the welfare, housing, employment and education provision which *must* provide reliable backup to all non-custodial penalties.

9 The book's final chapter argues the need for the development of a 'womanwise' penology based upon an open-ended feminist jurisprudence, and then finishes up by putting forward a strategy for the virtual abolition of women's imprisonment.

1
Women's crimes and women's imprisonment: current trends

In 1987 women constituted about 16 per cent of all persons found guilty or cautioned for indictable crimes, and about 23 per cent of those found guilty or cautioned for summary offences (Home Office, 1988a:84). In the same year, although females accounted for only 3.6 per cent of the total average daily prison population (Home Office, 1988b:17), the proportion of adult women convicted of indictable offences and sentenced to immediate imprisonment had risen from 3 per cent (in 1976) to 8 per cent (NACRO, 1989a). NACRO's 1987 analyses of women's imprisonment in England and Wales suggest both that the proportionate use of imprisonment for women had doubled in the previous ten years and that women tend to be sent to prison for less serious offences than men (NACRO, 1987a and 1987b). Indeed, whereas 19 per cent of women serving sentences in 1987 had no previous record of convictions, the proportion of adult males was only 7 per cent. However, although 'the largest [women's] offence group on June 30th 1987 was theft, handling, fraud and forgery, . . . the proportion of the population accounted for by this offence group (34 per cent) was 6 percentage points lower' than in June 1986. By contrast, the number of imprisoned female drugs offenders was about 60 per cent higher than a year earlier, and 32 per cent of women serving sentences for drugs offences had no record of previous convictions (Home Office, 1988b:86).

But enough of facts and figures. However varied the interpretations of the statistics might be, one overriding claim *can* be made: that during the last decade women in the criminal justice system have become much more visible – as crime victims, offenders, and as prisoners. In what ways, then, can the 'women, crime and imprisonment' scene be expected to change in the next decade? The Home Office is in little doubt. In April 1989 it predicted that by 1997 the average daily population of female prisoners will have increased by at least 400 on the 1988 figure of 1,800 (Home Office, 1989a). *The major contention of this book is that unless radical steps are immediately taken to reduce the female prison population and eventually abolish women's imprisonment in its present form, more and more women are likely to be imprisoned in the future.* As the arguments for reduction and abolition will be detailed in Chapter 5, I will now only outline what I see as being likely retrogressive trends in the next decade.

1 More women are likely to be imprisoned in the future

Although it would be unduly pessimistic to argue that proportionately there will be massive increases in the numbers of British women turning to crime in the next ten years, present trends in sentencing suggest that more of those who do will be given custodial sentences. This is primarily because, given present social trends, more of those coming before the courts are likely to be in those social categories which we *know* influence sentencing, i.e. more women are likely to have histories of childhood institutionalization (see Carlen, 1987 and 1988), more are likely to be divorced, and more are likely to have their children in residential Care. Additional factors contributing to an increase in the use of custody for women are likely to be (1) the present trend in sentencing which in 1984 resulted in a 50 per cent increase in women receiving immediate custody (Seear and Player, 1986); (2) the financial cuts which have resulted in the closing down (or the moving up market to deal with a more 'savable' middle-class clientele) of non-custodial facilities which previously kept at least some homeless, mentally ill, alcoholic (or otherwise addicted) offenders out of prison; and (3) the increasing use by psychiatrists of the concept 'personality disorder' to refuse hospital admission to offenders who are then imprisoned (Carlen, 1983a).

Some increase in the numbers of women charged with offences can also be expected, the major influencing factors here being: (1) the continuing deterioration in the general economic position of women in Britain; (2) the increase in drug-related offences; (3) increased regulation of prostitution as a result of AIDS-related fears; and (4) the knock-on effects of imprisonment itself that result in the narrowing of legitimate options each time a woman is incarcerated (see Rosenbaum, 1981; Carlen, 1988).

In both the US and the UK the economic position of women in general has rapidly deteriorated in the 1980s (US Dept. of Labor, 1985; Glendinning, 1987). This, combined with the immense increase in the numbers of lone mothers bringing up their children in poverty, may well lead to an increasing number of women feeling justified in breaking the law in order to keep their children fed, clothed and with a roof over their head. The crimes most easily available to them are shoplifting, fiddling social security, and prostitution (see Cook, 1987; Edwards, 1987).

2 At the same time – and also related to the increasing economic marginalization of women – there is likely to be an increase in the number of female drug users, a proportion of whom will become offenders as a result of their addiction

Although there is a growing body of research in England which suggests that the relationships between addiction and criminal activity (other than possession) are very complex (see Pearson *et al.*, 1986; Auld *et al.*, 1986; and Carlen, 1988), the US Dept. of Justice recently reported that 'almost one third of all inmates of state prisons were under the influence of an illegal drug or had drunk very heavily just before they had committed the crimes for which they were incarcerated' (Gropper, 1985). These last figures were not broken down into male and female rates, and in any case official statistics reveal only arrests for drug offences rather than *drug-related* crimes. None the less, a recent survey (US Dept. of Justice, 1987) in California showed that 29.8 per cent of women's felony arrests had followed drug violations, whilst some staff in the Californian jails for women claimed that 90 per cent of their inmates had committed offences in order to fund their regular engagement in substance abuse. Furthermore, present campaigns in Britain, aimed at both increasing the chances of drunken drivers being caught *and* increasing the likelihood of their being mandatorily imprisoned upon conviction, are likely, if successful, to bring increasing numbers of women into the courts and the prisons – as has already happened in the United States following the successful campaigning of MADD (Mothers Against Drinking and Driving).

3 Increased links between drug addiction and prostitution could also result in increasing regulation of prostitution as a consequence of growing fears about the sexual transmission of AIDS

At present, several English commentators argue that, because a majority of prostitute women insist on their clients using condoms, women engaging in prostitution fall into a low-risk category in relation to the transmission of AIDS. Yet this argument could be less plausible if there were to be an increase in the numbers of women turning to prostitution in order to fund a drug habit. If the drug-dependent prostitute woman is seen to be less likely to be concerned with 'safe sex' and more concerned with 'turning a quick trick', public demand for closer regulation of prostitution may increase.

Finally, and to conclude these depressing predictions, I have to point out that prisons feed off their own product. At present, British women come out of penal custody into a world that has even less to offer them than the prison itself, as the following statistics from the *Children in Danger Factfile* indicate.

'Over one and a half million children are being brought up in one parent families. In 1985 the average weekly income of one parent families was less than half (45%) of two parent families.' 86 per cent of one parent families are headed by women.

(National Children's Home, 1988:8, 7)

'In 1986, 1,140,000 families were on supplementary benefit – an increase of 137% since 1979.'

(ibid.:32)

In 1986 Building Societies repossessed 21 thousand homes.

In 1986 109,000 families were homeless and in priority need.

Confronted by such levels of deprivation it is not surprising that the many women who come out of prison jobless, homeless and penniless frequently give up the battle to survive in poverty-stricken respectability, drift into addiction or crime again and are then returned once more to gaol. And why shouldn't they be, you might ask. The answers are relatively simple.

1 Studies of sentencing suggest that the majority of women go to prison not because of the seriousness of their crime but because of a sentencing logic that discriminates against certain categories of women. (See Edwards, 1984 for an overview.)
2 Recent statistics released by the Home Office (1989b) suggest that disproportionate numbers of black women are sent to prison while other studies (e.g. NACRO, 1986a; Genders and Player, 1989) suggest that there are a number of factors throughout the criminal justice system which discriminate against black people.
3 As the majority of women remanded in custody eventually receive a non-custodial sentence (Casale, 1989) it is arguable that they were unnecessarily remanded in custody in the first place.
4 Mentally ill women and those with addictions receive no help in prison (Carlen, 1985; Casale, 1989) and the disciplinary regimes are likely to aggravate rather than ameliorate their problems (Carlen, 1983a; Mandaraka-Sheppard, 1986).
5 Imprisonment is a process that is counterproductive in terms of crime reduction as it increases the likelihood of some prisoners reoffending upon release. On its present scale, therefore, imprisonment cannot be part of a rational crime reduction policy (Home Office, 1988c).
6 Imprisonment in itself so aggravates any already existing problems which women have upon their reception into custody, that penal incarceration can be justified only as an exceptional measure – either to keep extremely dangerous offenders out of circulation or to punish particularly evil crimes.

Women in prison: general causes for concern

In the next chapter I shall be describing some of the better education and pre-release schemes in the women's prisons together with some of those aspects of women's imprisonment which undermine the rehabilitative intent of the educative and resettlement projects. In Chapter 2, therefore, I shall be discussing: the disgraceful plight of mentally ill women in prison; the failure of prisons to do anything constructive for prisoners with addictions; the lack of a comprehensive programme of pre-release courses for short-term prisoners; the neglect of the needs of foreign women due to be deported at the end of their sentences; the appalling lack of throughcare – especially for younger women and short-termers; and the punitive disciplinary regimes which annually result in disproportionately more female than male prisoners facing disciplinary charges (Home Office, 1988b; NACRO, 1989b). Yet there are other causes for concern in relation to women's imprisonment and they include: the long distances at which women are imprisoned from their home areas; medical services for women in prison; conditions at Risley Remand Centre; and conditions in Durham 'H' Wing, the maximum security block for females.

1 The long distances at which women are imprisoned from their homes

The relatively small numbers of women in the penal system result in many of them being held in prisons and remand centres hundreds of miles from their homes (see Chapter 2, p. 18 for a list of the women's penal establishments). Consequently, many do not receive visits from their children and other family members and friends. Even probation officers and lawyers are frequently reluctant to undertake long journeys for only short interviews with their clients. It was to remedy this disadvantage suffered by imprisoned women that Seear and Player (1986) recommended separate female sections within existing men's prisons. However, as Sylvia Casale has recently pointed out:

> The danger of sexual exploitation and the claustrophobic effect of extremely small wings for women prisoners are two of the disadvantages which must be weighed against the distress and damage caused by dislocation. This is a question on which emotions run high. There has as yet been no detailed and dispassionate analysis of the practical and political implications of these two less than ideal options.
>
> (Casale, 1989:32)

2 Medical services for women in prison

There has been a general concern about prison medicine and the lack of facilities for physically and mentally ill prisoners for years (see Gunn *et al.*, 1978; Coggan and Walker, 1982; Smith, 1984; Prison Reform Trust, 1985). The particular anxieties about women and prison health care have mainly been related to: the high dosages of psychotropic drugs which until the early 1980s were disproportionately administered to female prisoners (see Shaw, 1985:5); the lack of sympathy towards 'women's ailments' manifested by prison doctors (O'Dwyer *et al.*, 1987); the level of care given to women during pregnancy and after childbirth (GLC Women's Committee, 1986); the lack of specialized programmes for women defined as having personality disorders (Carlen, 1983a and 1985); the unhygienic conditions which menstruating women, pregnant women, and nursing mothers sometimes have to suffer, e.g. in solitary confinement or during long periods of 'lock up' occasioned by staff shortages (GLC Women's Committee, 1986); and the less than satisfactory level of care given to women with suicidal tendencies (see Benn and Ryder-Tchaikovsky, 1983). Despite recent agitation about the conditions in Holloway's C1 psychiatric unit and the recommendations for radical changes made by two reports (Home Office, 1985a; Clare and Thompson, 1985), in 1989 Sylvia Casale recorded that 'the new unit for C1 is still in the planning stage' (Casale, 1989:20). Current concerns about Risley Remand Centre and Durham 'H' Wing also have health implications (see below).

3 Risley Remand Centre

1988 saw the publication of the Chief Inspector's Report on HM Remand Centre, Risley, 'the only Remand Centre accepting young and adult inmates of both sexes' (Home Office, 1988d:7). At the time of the inspection 'the Centre had certified normal accommodation for 608 (514 males and 94 females) but actually contained 956 inmates (831 males and 125 females)' (ibid.). The Report paid particular attention to the area of suicide prevention and although in the main the women's unit was not so heavily criticized as the males' sections of the Centre, the following observations were made concerning women in the hospital wing or those specially located because of 'mental or personality problems' (ibid.:33):

> On the female side there were three separate accommodation areas for inmates located under segregation/punishment rules. E1 landing was the main area with 14 ordinary and two special cells. The majority of inmates on this landing were not located under these rules but were people with some mental, or personality problems who required closer supervision. . . . The routine/regime was basic but the level of care was excellent.
>
> (ibid.:33)

> Between 1st February 1987 and 30th January 1988 216 inmates were notified as possibly suicidal by the police or wings. They were all put into single cells. A Medical Officer told us that they do follow paragraph 37 of C1 3/1987 by admitting inmates to dormitory or shared accommodation and not putting them in isolation. However, the Grade V and the SMO told us that this was not so and that patients were invariably admitted to single cells. Exactly the same happened in the women's hospital.
>
> (ibid.:51)

We are not told how many of the 'possibly suicidal' inmates were women, but we do know that within a year of the Report's publication in April 1988 two women on remand at Risley had hanged themselves. One had been an addict withdrawing from heroin. The other had been remanded on burglary charges and was found hanged just one hour after being admitted.

4 Durham 'H' Wing

'H' Wing at Durham Prison housed male prisoners until 1971 when it was closed after two Reports (Home Office, 1966 and 1968) had concluded that it was unfit for use as a men's maximum security wing. Three years later it was reopened to house top security female prisoners. In 1989 a Report commissioned by Women in Prison, the Prison Reform Trust, the Howard League for Penal Reform and the National Council for Civil Liberties was made by Anthony Lester QC and Pamela J. Taylor. Among their conclusions were the following:

1 'Women in H Wing are being treated less favourably in important respects than they would be treated if they were male long-sentence or Category A prisoners, as regards some facilities and services, and it is strongly arguable that their unequal treatment is unlawful' (Lester and Taylor, 1989:5).
2 'The single most distressing internal problem for the women is the sanitation arrangements. H. Wing is still archaic, with no integral sanitary facilities in the cells' (ibid.:6).
3 'The absence of natural light and sunshine in H Wing is not likely to be conducive to mental or physical wellbeing' (ibid.:7).
4 'Time constraints on women are excessive' (ibid.:8).
5 'The amount of time allowed for exercise is manifestly insufficient, especially given the cramped conditions and limited work and educational facilities in H Wing' (ibid.:8).
6 'If H Wing were to remain as it is, without radical improvement we would recommend that it should be closed as soon as possible. In spite of the welcome changes in the past two or three years, women of H Wing are subjected to a poverty of environment and facilities unacceptable in a prison system committed to the civilised and humane objectives defined for the Prison Service by the Director General' (ibid.:11).

However, the Report's authors finally concluded that the scheduled building programme for 'H' Wing, together with the proposed new strategy for women lifers, should improve conditions considerably. It is to be hoped, therefore, that such improvements will have been made by the time this book is published.

2
Prisons: preparing women for release

Her Majesty's Prison Service serves the public by keeping in custody those committed by the courts. Our duty is to look after them with humanity and to help them lead law-abiding and useful lives in custody and after release.

(C.J. Train, Director, Her Majesty's Prison Service, November 1988)

If society genuinely wants to reduce recidivism, preparation for release must become a major priority for the prison system.

(Clive Soley, MP, 1986)

We hope eventually to extend pre-release courses to remand prisoners, because many of the problems prisoners confront when they go *out* are the ones that caused them to *come in* – losing their accommodation, losing their job. We hope to run courses that will limit the damage imprisonment causes. We find that women's main concern prior to release is with personal relationships, then with accommodation. Both men and women are often less concerned about work – because they were unemployed before they came in and they don't have high expectations of work being available when they get out. The full title of the courses is Pre-Release and Social Skills – to help them cope when they get out. *Not* reform and *not* rehabilitation, but more *survival* skills, that's what we're talking about.

(Senior official, Prison Department, 1989, his emphases)

In order to keep them out you actually have to give them something *outside*. Otherwise, a life of surviving in there seems preferable to life out here where there's just nothing.

(Josie O'Dwyer, ex-prisoner, in Carlen, 1988:137, emphasis added)

Odd as it may seem to have a chapter on women's prisons in a book investigating alternatives to custody, such a dimension is necessary because a woman's experience of imprisonment crucially affects her prospects on release. Too often that experience is damaging and debilitating (see Carlen, 1983a and 1988; Hicks and Carlen, 1985; O'Dwyer and Carlen, 1985). Therefore, though I agree with Genders and Player (1987) who have argued that 'an examination of first principles is called for in order to produce new directions for change,' this chapter will examine current educational, training and pre-release programmes with a view to assessing their relevance to post-release needs. The main arguments will be that:

1 Until prison regimes for women are fundamentally altered (and preferably by the abolition of women's imprisonment in its present form – see Chapter 5) piece-meal reforms will probably generate more tensions and contradictions than they resolve.
2 Increased inequality and poverty in 1980s Britain has enabled official prison ideology to strengthen its claims to 'saving' women prisoners from the rigours and results of destitution outside prison. At the same time, the poverty-stricken living conditions which confront many women upon release are still invoked as both justifying women's imprisonment and absolving prisons from charges that their regimes atrophy rather than augment any survival skills which women might have had prior to incarceration.

The prisons

At the end of March 1989 convicted women prisoners were being held in six closed and three open prisons. Additionally, women on remand were held at Holloway and the Low Newton, Risley and Pucklechurch remand centres. At Durham women were held in one wing of the men's prison. Bullwood Hall, Cookham Wood, Holloway, Styal and New Hall were the closed women's prisons and/or youth custody centres. Askham Grange, Drake Hall and East Sutton Park were the open establishments. A new prison for women, Brock Hill, is scheduled to take its first prisoners in 1992.

During the latter part of 1987 and the first few months of 1988 I contacted seven of the women's establishments (excluding Durham, New Hall, Risley and Pucklechurch), requesting the governors either to allow me to visit the prison and interview the relevant staff about in-prison programmes expected to be beneficial to women upon release, or to allow staff to give me written information about such programmes. The governors of Askham Grange, Bullwood Hall, Cookham Wood and Drake Hall invited me to talk to staff in the prisons; East Sutton Park returned a completed questionnaire, Styal declined to participate in the research, and no reply was received from Holloway. In 1988 further information was given to me at an interview with a woman official at the Midland Regional Headquarters of the Prison Department in Birmingham, and in January 1989 I was updated on pre-release developments at national headquarters in London. Most of the information in this chapter comes from these sources, though it is supplemented by data taken from official, research and campaigning publications.

In writing about the prison programmes I shall be reporting first on the positive aspects – describing them as they were described to me. What is presented here, however, is not intended as a comprehensive overview of all education and pre-release innovations. In being selective I shall not be intending to imply that the programmes of establishments not mentioned are lacking in any way. Instead I shall merely be starting the discussion by describing *some* of the best work being done in the women's prisons. Then I will outline some of the countervailing tendencies (in the penal and criminal justice systems and in contemporary social and penal ideologies) which presently subvert the aims of the prisons' pre-release schemes. Finally, the many gaps in existing provision will be listed.

Education in women's prisons

Historically, the educational emphasis in women's prisons has been upon domesticity. Although Smith (1962:299) asserts that at least by 1957 'it was . . . acknowledged that women prisoners should be returned to society trained as efficient "housewives" rather than as efficient "housemaids"', as late as 1973 a Prison Department policy document (Home Office, 1973) was stressing that educational programmes for women should cover 'personal relationships, family life, home management, child rearing and other domestic topics' (Brown, 1982:113). According to Brown (ibid.) in 1977–8 a breakdown of class time in seven of the women's prisons gave priority to the teaching of topics classed as 'leisure activities' (See Table 2:1).

Table 2:1 Breakdown of class time in women's prisons 1977–8

	%
Leisure activities	27
Vocational and domestic training	19
Academic work	19
Remedial education	16
Social education	7
Typing and office skills	6
Hygiene and health	3
Physical education	3

(Figures from Brown, 1982)

Reports by Her Majesty's Chief Inspector of Prisons suggest that the picture has been slowly changing throughout the 1980s, though the sparse information concerning education in the Reports on some of the women's prisons does not suggest that educational provision has been given high priority in those establishments.

Table 2.2 1980s educational provision in seven women's penal establishments – as described in Reports of HM Inspector of Prisons

Date of report and reference	Institution	Educational provision
1981 (Home Office, 1981)	Cookham Wood (closed prison)	(1 page in Report.) Remedial classes in literacy, numeracy and craft skills; study courses in English and office skills; correspondence courses and Open University facilities; up to 2 hours physical education per week; vocational course in home economics. In preparation – a course in electronic wiring.
1984 (Home Office, 1984a)	Bullwood Hall (closed borstal at time of inspection (1982). Now closed prison and youth custody centre)	(Only 14 lines in Report on education.) The only information on actual courses was (1) 'There was a good daytime and evening educational programme which was well designed to meet the needs of the establishment' (p.11). (2) Six trainees took a training course in home economics.
1984 (Home Office, 1984b)	Pucklechurch (remand centre for males and females)	(½ page of Report but only 3 lines on provision for females.) 'The programme provided for the female inmates was limited by the lack of space but was reasonably balanced and well supported, although classes were liable to cancellation at short notice' (p. 14).
1985 (Home Office, 1985b)	Askham Grange (open prison)	(2 pages of Report.) Remedial literacy and commercial skills; childcare (for inmates in the mother and baby unit). A 'reasonably balanced programme of evening classes' per week. Vocational training courses in electronic wiring and home economics. Planned: City and Guilds courses for members of the works and garden parties; computer activities and science and mathematics based work 'when the roll permitted expansion' (p. 27).
1985 (Home Office, 1985c)	Holloway (closed prison)	(1¼ pages of Report.) 'Full range of daytime and evening classes ranging from basic remedial education . . . to Open University courses. Six Civilian Instructional Officers were engaged in the Skills Training Unit. . . . There were two Home Economics courses and another in Typewriting and Office Arts' (p.23).

Table 2.2 (cont'd)

Date of report and reference	Institution	Educational provision
1987 (Home Office, 1987)	East Sutton Park (open prison and youth custody centre)	(¾ page of Report.) Commercial skills course; academic provision for those studying for 'O' and 'A' levels; literacy and numeracy courses; art, craft, music, cookery, beauty care courses five evenings each week. Vocational courses in home economics and soft furnishings.
1988 (Home Office, 1988d)	Risley (remand centre for males and females)	(1 page in main body of Report on female education.) '. . . no formal accommodation for education but whenever possible the dining room was utilised. More often than not . . . even this meagre facility was frequently denied to inmates. In the female hospital there was one classroom that was used five mornings a week for approximately 14 inmates. . . . Classes were held in crafts and social skills' (p.42).

In 1988–9 the Education Department of Drake Hall was running a very comprehensive programme of daytime courses including computing, home economics, hairdressing, needlecraft, Look After Yourself (involving a range of 'pre-release' topics), social skills and basic English and maths. Two particularly innovative courses had also been newly introduced: the Dartington Hall course in speech and drama which had been quite remarkable in building up the self-confidence of some of the prisoners; and the Start Your Own Business course which, according to the Governor, had 'made many of the wives realize they should start answering back more'. A range of leisure activities (e.g. hair and beauty, yoga, pottery), skills (e.g. English, maths, psychology, French for beginners) and 'support' activities (e.g. alcohol users' group, heroin users' group, 'how the criminal justice system works' and religious discussions) were run in the evenings. At the time of my visit in March 1988 an industrial cleaning course was being planned.

Pre-release schemes in women's prisons

Pre-release schemes are already run at Askham Grange, Drake Hall, Styal, New Hall and Durham, and soon are to be started at Holloway. The aim is to get co-ordination between the different professional groups involved – probation, education, psychology and prison officers. In some establishments it's compulsory for young offenders and therefore there's 100 per cent attendance. In other establishments attendance can be as low as 10 per cent.

(Senior official, Prison Department, 1989)

Question: Do you run any specifically pre-release programmes?
No. As this is a small prison the needs of each inmate are considered individually, whether they are serving a long (including life) or a short sentence.
                              (Reply to questionnaire, East Sutton Park, 1988)

The pre-release course [at Sutton Park] which is known as the Personal and Home Management course runs for six weeks and is available to any women near the end of their sentence. . . . Many of the sessions covered on this course are covered by outside tutors, e.g. the local job centre and CAB, which is an advantage, the problem is that pre-release is not part of the prison regime so does not always happen.

                                                        (WPRC, 1989a:8)

Pre-release schemes are not being run at the moment.
                              (Probation officer, Cookham Wood, 1988)

Until recently Cookham Wood was the only women's prison where prison officers set up, organised and ran the pre-release course.

                                                        (WPRC, 1989a:6)

When I was investigating pre-release schemes in the women's prisons the most frequent comment I received was that 'it's all in the melting pot at the moment', followed either by comments relating to the industrial unrest occasioned by implementation of some of the changes involved in the Fresh Start programme (a Prison Department Prison Management Initiative – see Home Office, 1988e:43–4) or by reference to the difficulties of getting all the relevant professional groups working together. By spring 1988, however, Drake Hall already had a pre-release scheme in operation while Askham Grange's Pre-Release Employment Scheme (PRES) had been well established for several years.

In March 1988 the one week pre-release course at Drake Hall included a wide range of speakers from national and local organizations. The programme covered the following topics: repair and alteration of clothes, family planning, health education, Samaritans, preparation of a meal, first aid, DHSS, consumer protection, survival, marriage guidance, budgetting, housing, Apex-job finding and keeping, preparation of a CV, etc., and good grooming. Additionally, three other courses could claim to prepare prisoners for release. A compulsory two week Life and Social Skills course for Youth Custody Trainees included (amongst others) sessions on finding somewhere to live, form filling, 'know your rights', sexually transmitted diseases and job seeking. The Looking After Yourself (Lay) course run by the Education Department aimed to help women prepare themselves for returning to life outside the prison and dealt with communication skills, health (both physical and mental), job hunting, leisure pursuits available at minimum cost, and help agencies and self-help groups. Finally, the Education Department's Access course provided 'opportunity for potential students to discover if they could benefit from and cope with the demands of a course of study in a college of further or higher education' (Drake Hall Prison Education Department, 1988).

Pre-Release Employment Scheme Hostel (PRES)

At the time of the 1985 inspection of Askham Grange's Pre-Release Employment Scheme Hostel, 'only four of 16 places were occupied, an under-utilisation of 75%' (Home Office, 1985b). When I visited in 1988, however, there were 16 hostellers in residence, 37 women having entered the scheme during 1987, with only 9 having to be removed during that year because of unsuitability. In 1988 the PRES scheme was open to applications from all female prisoners serving a sentence of 18 months or more while all life sentence prisoners *had* to complete their programme on the scheme. Once at the hostel, women were allowed 6 weeks in which to find work, becoming eligible for two late passes per week after they had been in residence for 4 weeks and home leave after they had been in employment for 4 weeks. Each resident occupied a study bedroom to which she held the key. Very flexible working hours (including night work) were permitted. Wages were handed over in total to the Hostel Warden who, after deducting board and lodging and returning £9 spending money plus fares to and from work to the hosteller, deposited the remainder in the woman's account. Withdrawals (e.g. for clothing, hairdressing, presents for children) could be made upon application.

When I visited Drake Hall and Askham Grange – the only two prisons where I spent any time with the Education Officers – I was very impressed by the work being done and by the enthusiasm of all the prison personnel with whom I talked. At Drake Hall, for instance, a prison officer gave me a very detailed explanation of the industrial work available and of the problems encountered by Drake Hall's many non-English speaking prisoners. At Askham Grange the Hostel Warden, a probation officer and an education officer all spent time explaining some of the rewards and difficulties associated with their work. Yet, when I turned to the *Prison Statistics England and Wales, 1987* to obtain an overview of work, education and pre-release schemes in women's prisons, figures were provided only for the men's. 'Corresponding figures for female establishments are not available' (Home Office, 1988b). Same old story.

Mother and baby units

Sussex University has produced the first firm research evidence of the effects of a mother's imprisonment on very young children.

The study, commissioned by the Home Office, monitored the physical and psychological development of babies between one and 18 months old who accompanied their mothers into mother-and-baby units at three different prisons.

Their development was compared with that of babies of similar age who were separated from their mothers and cared for by relatives or others while the mother was in prison.

The research found little difference in babies' development over a short period, but there was evidence of a gradual decline in cognitive development (learning ability) and locomotor development (crawling, walking, etc) in babies who stayed in the mother-baby unit for four or more months.

Morning Star, Tuesday, 4 April 1989,
referring to the work of Dr Lisa Catan

The position of mothers and young babies in prison underlines the urgent need to find alternatives to women's imprisonment. For, as Adriana Caudrey pointed out in a 1987 *Observer* article (4 October), women prisoners entitled to have their babies with them 'are frequently those sentenced for comparatively minor offences, some of which could attract non-custodial sentences.' In the meantime, while some women do continue to keep their babies in prison, to what extent do the regimes in England's three mother and baby units at Askham Grange, Styal and Holloway prisons give mothers and children a good start in life?

The three mother and baby units provide a total of only 39 places; 13 at Askham Grange, 14 at Styal and 12 at Holloway. 'Mothers are not eligible for the mother and baby units at Holloway and Styal if their child will be more than 9 months old by their earliest date of release, or 18 months at Askham Grange' (NACRO, 1988a). Criticisms directed against the units have typically related to: the long hours that mothers and babies spend confined to one room; the strict supervision which prevents women from developing their own baby routines; and the separation of the babies from men, other relatives and the extra stimulation of life beyond the prison walls. In open conditions, of course, some of these criticisms can be met. At Askham Grange, for example, mothers take their babies for a weekly walk round the village and the older babies have outings to a local nursery and to the homes of relatives. Yet it could be argued (and often *is* by ex-prisoner mothers) that the prison regimes of all the units (1) fail to allow the women to develop their own methods of baby care; (2) reduce what little confidence some of them already have in their ability to cope with the baby outside prison; and (3) induce tension when mothers have methods of childrearing and baby diets imposed upon them with which they disagree. Counterarguments involving assertions that physically and materially the babies of mothers living in poverty-stricken conditions outside get off to a better start in prison may indeed be true, but it should be a sobering truth which admits that in 1980s Britain some women are still so destitute that the prison provides the best shelter for them and their infants (see Chapter 3). At the end of this chapter I shall be analysing some of the discursive contradictions and continuities which shape contemporary debates about mothers in prison. Till then, the words of John Hunter, a previous governor of Askham Grange, sufficiently and succinctly summarize what is essentially wrong with every prison's mother and baby unit: 'It's not the sort of life every mother would choose to bring her baby

into. . . . Try as we might we can't make it a normal "outside" environment'
(NACRO, 1988a).

Links with outside

The strenuous campaigning by newly formed organizations struggling for a better
deal for women prisoners has, in the last few years, resulted in many more outside
groups being allowed into the women's establishments for welfare, educational and
entertainment purposes. Listings of the groups which in 1988 were visiting just
two of the prisons – Bullwood Hall and Cookham Wood – indicate the range of
services offered by voluntary groups. The African Prisoners' Association, Apex
Trust, the Black Female Prisoners' Scheme, the North London Education Trust,
Women in Prison and the Women Prisoners' Resource Centre visited at both
prisons. Additionally, Alcoholics Anonymous, the Citizens' Advice Bureau, the
Co-ordinated Accommodation Scheme, CAST, Rape Crisis Centre and the
Rastafarian Advisory Service visited at Bullwood Hall; the Kent Unit for the
Guidance of Ex-Offenders and the Langley House Trust visited at Cookham
Wood. (At both prisons my informants suggested that the visiting groups were so
numerous that they could not remember all of them.) The outside organizations
mentioned most frequently by prison personnel were NACRO, the Women
Prisoners' Resource Centre, the Black Female Prisoners' Scheme, Clean Break and
CAST (see Chapter 4 for detailed description of the work of Clean Break and
CAST).

NACRO

NACRO's already well-established pre-release services to prisoners have recently
been co-ordinated by the newly created Prisons Link Unit. Its work includes
distributing NACRO advice leaflets on housing, education and drug abuse; setting
up referral systems for interested prisoners to join NACRO education, training and
other community schemes; and providing information on recent changes in social
security and government employment and training schemes (Home Office, 1988e;
NACRO, 1988b). During 1987–8 'work with selected prisons included involvement with New Hall, a newly converted local prison for women' (NACRO,
1988b:19). Several complimentary remarks about NACRO were made by the
prison personnel I talked with, a teacher at Drake Hall for instance being particularly impressed by her experience that 'some NACROs [representatives from
specific projects] will come up for the day just to interview one girl.' In 1984
NACRO set up a separate project specifically for women prisoners – the Women
Prisoners' Resource Centre – and it was this agency to which my informants in the
women's prisons referred most frequently.

Women Prisoners' Resource Centre (WPRC)

'WPRC was established to help identify and meet the resettlement needs of women in prison who would be returning to London on their release' (WPRC, 1989a:2). WPRC workers therefore regularly visit the establishments where London women are mainly held (i.e. Holloway, Bullwood Hall, Cookham Wood, East Sutton Park, Durham, Drake Hall, Styal and Askham Grange). Upon request they also visit New Hall, Risley, Low Newton and Pucklechurch. WPRC workers visiting the prisons deal with queries about post-release housing, education, employment, welfare, social security, drugs problems, etc., by linking up prisoners with the relevant agencies or service providers outside. Arrangements for WPRC visits vary from prison to prison; for example, every two weeks sessions are held at Holloway where women are seen in the general visits room (ibid.:9), whereas monthly visits are paid to Bullwood where WPRC workers hold advice group sessions on the wings and also take part 'in the pre-release course which is jointly run by the probation and education departments in the prison' (ibid.:6). When I myself was interviewing prisoners in Bullwood in 1985 I was given glowing accounts of the work of WPRC. Women were particularly impressed by the efficient way in which WPRC was putting them in touch with organizations which actually could be seen to be delivering the goods in relation to at least some of their post-release needs. In 1989 WPRC produced a comprehensive Reception Pack covering such areas as housing, benefits, tax, debts, fines, pets, drugs, alcohol, health, employment, education, religion, legal aid and appeals, deportation, probation and the Rehabilitation of Offenders Act.

The Black Female Prisoners' Scheme

The Black Female Prisoners' Scheme was founded in 1983 at the same time as the Women in Prison organization. In 1986 the Home Office began to publish figures on the ethnic origins of prisoners (Home Office, 1986) and provisional data published in April 1989 showed that on 30 June 1988 at least 18.5 per cent of all female prisoners were of West Indian, Guyanese and African origin; at least 1.6 per cent were of Indian, Pakistani or Bangladeshi origin; and at least 3 per cent were of Chinese, Arab or mixed origin (Home Office, 1989b). In 1987–8 34 per cent of referrals to WPRC were black (WPRC, 1989a). It was the realization that there was a need for a separate service for black female offenders that resulted in the formation of the Black Female Prisoners' Scheme in 1983. Since then the Scheme has established a visiting programme in all the female penal establishments, an Education Unit that offers educational and social activities to all black female ex-offenders and single parents in the London area, and a welfare fund to assist financially both women in prison and those attending the Education Unit (Thomas-Crandon, 1988).

Prisoners' reports on education and preparation for release schemes

Women who have had experience of education courses in prison usually praise them. However, despite the impressive array of subjects on offer at some establishments the majority of prisoners, being short-termers, cannot take advantage of them. As they move from remand institution to the one (or more) where they are to serve sentence, they often find that all courses in the new establishment are already fully booked. Audrey Peckham's experience was typical:

> I had had the usual interview with the education people . . . but there wasn't much they could do for me. I was not staying long enough for Open University, and the other classes in which I might have been interested were fully booked.
>
> (Peckham, 1985)

When I asked a teacher at Drake Hall how many women were actually taking courses her guesstimate was 25 per cent. Six months later the Governor's was more optimistic but still only 40 per cent. Even when women are accepted for a course there are still many obstacles and countervailing forces, the main one at some women's prisons being prison officers' industrial action which so often involves refusal to escort prisoners to classes and other recreational activities. In addition, for prisoners above the statutory school leaving age (16+) prison education is a privilege not a right; it can always be terminated by disciplinary design (as part of a punishment) or by organization requirements (e.g. by the prisoner being moved to another prison) or by budgetary constraints. An ex-prisoner who obtained her degree in Cornton Vale prison in Scotland told of an experience I have heard also described by English prisoners.

> I'm often held up as a quite good example of what prison can do. I'm actually much more of an example of what can happen *despite* the system. Because the system at no point helped me. I did a lot of studying in prison, but I had to fight for it. And for the first three years of that study I was actually told, 'If you want to do this it's in your own time. And you must perform all the normal prison duties as we expect them to be done. . . .' I bloody well had to do it the hard way. They were *not* making it easy for me – I had to bargain for what I got.
>
> (Emma, ex-prisoner, in Bardsley, 1987:93)

In 1985 NACRO surveyed (by questionnaire) 29 people to find out what kind of pre-release preparation they had received in prison (NACRO, 1986b). The length of time they had spent in prison on their last sentence had ranged from 13 days to 14 years of a life sentence. Eleven of the respondents were women. The following comment by one of the respondents (gender not given) is typical of those which ex-prisoners still make about the *ad hoc* nature of many prison programmes.

In the one I've just come out of, they were on about starting an Alcoholics Anonymous group in there. I was in there 7 months, and they said this when I was on my 2 week reception. So I thought right, and went through my whole 7 months thinking: right, they will start it soon – and they never bothered. Same with drugs. They never bothered with that – they did a week's course and only 10 could go on it. Well it's no use to you. You've got 200 in that prison.

(NACRO, 1986b)

The authors of the Report concluded that 'help on different topics came from predictable sources but was *ad hoc*. There was no evidence that any of the people in the sample had been through a systematic planned programme of release' (ibid.).

The penal context of education and pre-release schemes in the women's prisons

Without exception, the pre-release and education course tutors to whom I spoke were enthusiastic, innovative and very committed to their work. Yet there are other dimensions to prison life, seemingly higher priorities than those of educating and equipping the prisoner for release, and these countervailing factors tend to subvert – almost to the point of destruction – many of the prison's more positive influences. First, there are the absences – the lack of adequate programmes specifi- cally designed to meet the needs of the mentally ill, drug abusers, short-termers, young people aged 15–20, and deportees. Second, in the case of many prisoners the concept of throughcare – a continuity of probation care while the woman is in gaol – is more honoured in the breach than the observance. Third, there are organiza- tional and administrative exigencies which can result in cancellation of classes, interrupt the programmes of individual prisoners or otherwise undermine the educational and pre-release work. Fourth, there are a number of contemporary ideologies in relation to women's imprisonment which work against a radical commitment to courses, activities and penal regimes which might equip women to live more satisfying and independent lives upon release. And finally, even if like Emma (above), women prisoners do come through triumphant, the life that awaits them outside the prison walls will often be so poverty stricken that they give up the struggle to keep out of trouble – and land up in gaol again.

Gaps in provision for women prisoners

1 Failure to meet the needs of the mentally ill

Failure to cater for the needs of the mentally ill is not peculiar to women's prisons (see Carlen, 1986). In men's prisons, too, provision is woefully inadequate, while the Chief Inspector's most recent Report on Risley Remand Centre (for young adults of both sexes) noted a 'shocking . . . disregard of Circular Instruction

3/1987 which laid down in detail the steps to be taken to look out for suicidal tendencies' (Home Office, 1988d:3). In 1985 and 1986 Holloway's C1 psychiatric unit attracted a good deal of notoriety because of its unsuitability for the highly disturbed women located there (see Home Office, 1985a; Clare and Thompson, 1985; O'Dwyer et al., 1987), while Her Majesty's Chief Inspector of Prisons noted in the 1985 Report on Holloway that when his team checked the medical histories of incoming prisoners they found that 'around 40% of admissions had a history of mental illness in some form while some 30% had been assessed as potentially suicidal' (Home Office, 1985c).

Prison personnel will usually argue that there are many women in prison who, because of their mental state, should instead be in hospital. Yet such a readiness to define so many (maybe too many?) women prisoners as mentally ill has not led to serious consideration of the extent to which prison regimes themselves might either increase a woman's mental stress or induce behaviour which can appear to be completely crazed (see O'Dwyer and Carlen, 1985). Furthermore, there are still no units for women which are equivalent to the men's psychotherapeutic units at Grendon Underwood and Wormwood Scrubs Prisons.

Audrey Peckham was on remand accused of incitement to murder when she sought help from a prison psychiatrist.

> He barely glanced at me as I came in and said something like, 'Well, you shouldn't have done that, should you?' I replied, 'I didn't do it. Can I tell you about it?' He actually said, 'If you must,' and looked at his watch. I could say nothing after that.
>
> (Peckham, 1985:52)

Since 1985 many women have described to me experiences of prison psychiatry which were very similar to Ms Peckham's. Others, particularly young women, have recounted how the boredom and tension generated by being locked up in a cell alone for long periods had culminated in them either smashing up the cell or slashing their wrists, faces or other parts of their bodies. Surely it is not in the public interest for mentally and emotionally disturbed women to be sentenced to penal regimes which send them out less able to cope than before they were imprisoned? As Hilary Allen (1987a, 1987b and 1989) has demonstrated, many women who have been convicted of serious crimes of violence are sentenced to non-custodial penalties. It should not be necessary, therefore, repeatedly to incarcerate women who are more of a nuisance than a threat, whose main offence is that because no one can make much sense of their behaviour, they successfully avoid incorporation into the professional scripts of the criminal justice gatekeepers (probation officers, social workers and psychiatrists) whose intervention might have saved them from prison (Worrall, 1989). These are the women who are often assessed as unsuitable for 'education'. As far as pre-release courses are concerned, it is absurd for the Prison Department to suggest that a one or two week pre-release course will limit or reverse the further damage that imprisonment inflicts on already disturbed people. Mentally ill and emotionally damaged women should by and large *not* be in prison and when, because of the seriousness of their crime, they *have* to be locked up, they should be held in an entirely different type of establishment to those in which women are currently imprisoned.

2 Failure to meet the needs of drug (including alcohol) abusers

> There is little doubt if you speak to anybody who works with prisoners that the number of women in prison with a history of drug or alcohol abuse has increased and is estimated at between 50% and 80%.
>
> (WPRC, 1989a)

Some sentencers appear to think that in prison women are helped with their addictions. This is not so. Prisoners withdrawing from illegal drugs are usually kept in the hospital wing during the period of withdrawal, but they receive counselling only if they are in an establishment that allows them access to workers from an outside rehabilitation agency. Some women are grateful for the forced abstention from drugs which their custodial sentences impose upon them, others think (and talk) continually about the 'fix' they will have as soon as they get out. Illegal drugs can be obtained by imprisoned women desperate (or bored) enough to take the risk.

Many women in prison do not express a readiness to give up their addictions, but for those who do the post-release prospects are bleak. Projects like the North London Education Project as well as some charitable accommodation schemes will not take women with a recent history of drug abuse and even some drug rehabilitation projects will not take women straight from prison. At the same time, because most of the rehab projects are mixed, many women (especially those who have been physically or sexually abused by men) will not consider attending them, and the projects which will on occasion take women with children are few and far between. The most useful pre-release scheme for women indicating a strong desire to abandon their habits would be the setting up of an all women 'bridging' project for prisoners and ex-prisoners only. This should be an 'open' rehabilitation project in which women could elect to spend the last months of their sentence and then continue at the same project upon release. (See Chapter 5 for further development of this proposal, together with discussion of a similar scheme in California.)

3 Failure to meet the needs of short-term prisoners

Fine defaulters and other women imprisoned for very short periods at a time presently suffer most of the ill-effects of imprisonment without benefiting from the education or pre-release courses. Short-term recidivist prisoners may spend a considerable part of their lives in custody and yet be amongst the most neglected of the prison population. I was therefore glad to be told by a senior official in the Prison

Department in 1988 that, as a result of the 1987 Criminal Justice Bill's provision for a unified custodial sentence for young offenders, the educational needs of all short-term prisoners were then under review. But these short-termers should NOT be in prison at all. (See Chapter 5 for further discussion of categories of offender and prisoners who should not be in custody.)

4 Deportees

> Women in British prisons who will be deported at the end of their sentences are some of the most neglected and isolated women within the prison system.
>
> (WPRC, 1989a)

Many deportees face long sentences for the illegal importation of drugs, speak little or no English, have no idea of their legal rights and are often totally confused as to the exact nature of their offence. One prison officer at Drake Hall was convinced that some of them served their sentences without really understanding how they came to be there at all.

> I'm sure that some know *exactly* what they're doing but others have little idea at all. We're now beginning to see ones coming back who've been here before. They've served their sentence, been deported, and come back; so it's no deterrent.

Aysha Tarzi, Foreign Affairs Co-ordinator in the Inner London Probation Service, conducted a survey of foreign offenders in prison and came to similar conclusions.

> Often drug smugglers are women who are not normally criminal. Nigerian women come back again and again and it's difficult to believe that they don't know what they're doing. But with Asian women they often do it through sheer desperation. They take the risk because of their poverty. They don't want their embassies to know they're in prison so they're very isolated.

At Drake Hall ESL (English as a second language) teachers from a local college hold classes for foreign prisoners. A Foreign Prisoners' Information Pack has been developed by Ms Tarzi and has been put on offer to all prisons. This pack, funded by the Inner London Probation Service, has been translated into sixteen languages: French, German, Spanish, Dutch, Italian, Greek, Chinese, Vietnamese, Turkish, Iranian, Arabic, Hindi, Gurgerati, Punjabi, Bengali, and Urdo. Importantly, as well as giving information about the dos and don'ts of prison life, it also has a section on the questions (and range of possible answers) asked of prisoners on reception. However, although in Summer 1988 the pack was known to be in use in over 40 penal establishments, at that time Ms Tarzi was uncertain as to whether the relevant pack was on offer to *all* foreign women in English prisons. In any case it could only be of limited use to illiterate prisoners.

In sum, it seems that much more needs to be done for deportees. They should be helped to keep in touch with families at home. Counselling should be provided about the nature of their offence and the likely consequences of repeating it. Prison staff should receive training concerning the cultures of the different countries from which deportees come. With the agreement of individuals, attempts should be made to link deportees with the relevant church or other ethnic minority organizations whose representatives should be encouraged to visit (and speak for) them.

5 Throughcare

Guidance on prisoner throughcare issued in 1986 stressed that responsibility for meeting the welfare needs of prisoners should be shared between prison officers, probation officers and other specialists. . . . The new guidance on regimes for young offenders stresses that throughcare is integral to all aspects of the regime.

(Home Office, 1988e:26)

A constant complaint of probation officers working in the prisons was that their colleagues outside did not visit prisoners often enough. Usually they knew why. In recent years some services have had to impose financial cuts which have resulted in less money being available for distant prison visits. Some probation officers – though by no means a majority, it was thought – themselves give low priority to prison visiting. At Manchester one male senior probation officer could give an excellent account of the throughcare available to clients.

We have one officer especially for throughcare who will visit all the men and women in custody and informally we have a minimum standards policy which means we operate a very thorough throughcare scheme and visit at regular intervals. Presently we have 3 women at Askham Grange and 2 at Styal. They've all been visited.

Probation officers at Cookham Wood and Bullwood Hall could, from a different vantage point, give a more comprehensive picture.

Probation officers don't always come regularly and when they do come they haven't always done their preparation. Some write, but the girls would prefer them to visit. Some probation officers come a lot to visit the older prisoners and do a lot of work with their families. Some younger prisoners don't even know the name of the officer who wrote their social inquiry report; others have a bad relationship with their probation officer anyhow. Ideally the officer should write and ask if the woman wants a visit, but those who do are the exception rather than the rule. When someone is in prison, probation officers often give priority to those outside who've got terrible problems and at least the person in prison is safe – so then the prisoners tend to get passed over. Long-termers usually get a good service and throughcare works best for them. If I worked in the field again I think I'd make more effort [to visit prisoners] now that I've seen how important a visit is.

(Probation officer, Cookham Wood)

Nowadays many more people are coming here [Bullwood Hall] from London and they *will* be visited by a probation officer. Outside that area some proba-tion areas won't finance an officer to come. One woman I can think of had a six year sentence but she didn't get a visit from her probation officer. Those who write to their probation officers *do* get replies. Personally, I think throughcare was accorded low priority by the probation service several years ago. ACOP has been told often enough that throughcare needs to be given more priority.

(Senior probation officer, Bullwood Hall)

Until all agencies both within and beyond the prison walls have a co-ordinated throughcare policy not constantly undermined by economic cuts, pre-release schemes will continue to be seen by prisoners as but drops in the ocean of neglect and poverty that engulfs many of them upon release.

Organizational and administrative exigencies which subvert education and other positive elements in the women's prisons

1 Inadequate resources

A constant theme in the Chief Inspector's Reports on the women's prisons has been that educational classes are held in cramped conditions and are sometimes under-resourced.

The programme provided for the female inmates was limited by lack of space. [Pucklechurch]

(Home Office, 1984b)

The education department was in cramped accommodation which was in-adequate for the normal population of the borstal. [Bullwood Hall]

(Home Office, 1984a)

The child-care centre and pre-release programme had been introduced to meet national policy and local management wishes. Neither had attracted extra funding and there was evidence that the education budget would soon be overspent. [Askham Grange]

(Home Office, 1985b)

Although the education programme was well balanced and made a major contribution to the inmates' regime it was constrained to some extent by the available accommodation. [East Sutton Park]

(Home Office, 1987)

The senior probation officer at Bullwood Hall thought that accommodation and funding of the outside groups were totally inadequate and that if prisons recognized the worth of the services provided from outside, some kind of central funding should be made available.

> Outside groups come in but we don't have appropriate accommodation. For instance, we might have AA [Alcoholics Anonymous] in here plus a welfare visit going on next door – all in unsuitable conditions and we have to move people about. Maybe the group goes into my office (because that's the only room that's big enough) and I'm reduced to carrying chairs from room to room. Not that I mind doing that but I'm supposed to be the Senior Welfare Officer – liaising with groups, running groups and so on. If they want us to do the job they must be seen to give us the resources. As far as outside groups are concerned they only get mileage and subsistence. We seem to expect them to do a great deal for nothing. When the GLC folded many groups folded. Now they're always phoning us and saying, 'We can't come, our funding's gone.'

2 Industrial action and staff shortages

> Classes were liable to cancellation at short notice. [Pucklechurch]
>> (Home Office, 1984b)

> The evening programme was frequently curtailed because there were no staff to unlock, escort and supervise the trainees. [Bullwood Hall]
>> (Home Office, 1984a)

> Classes were . . . frequently liable to cancellation because there were insufficient discipline staff to supervise the education area . . . even when classes were being held the number of inmates allowed to attend them at any one time when two discipline officers were on duty was restricted to 40. This was at the insistence of the local branch of the Prison Officers' Association [POA] who apparently took the view that to permit a large number of prisoners in the education area might constitute a risk to security and control. [Holloway]
>> (Home Office, 1985c)

At the time of my interviews with senior Prison Department staff in 1988 and 1989 I was assured that, as a result of the implementation of the Fresh Start proposals for the complete overhaul and reorganization of prison officer work schedules, officers would in future have more time to ensure that all classes run according to plan. However, it seems that until there are better industrial relations within the prison service and until there is a Minimum Standards Code specifying a general right of prisoners to attend classes in which they have enrolled, inmates will continue to be the main losers in the continuing power struggle between the POA and the Prison Department.

3 Lack of central direction and co-ordination

> People who are in a position to provide backup services do not do so. On that

board over there you'll see notices from different organizations and in some
way we're virtually saturated with outside resources. But no account is taken
of the need to service those organizations. As far as this institution is concerned, they'll let people come in but as soon as anything goes wrong they're
on the phone to criticize. There's no organization or communication. This
morning, for instance, the CAB is coming in and I'd already given the names
of the women who wanted to see them to the wing officers. But when I sent
for them they [prisoners] had been sent off to work. It's not obstruction (I
hope!). More, lack of organization. Yesterday a senior member of staff
phoned me asking about the Apex Trust. I said, 'There's a poster on the
notice board on the wing.' 'No there isn't,' she said. 'Then it's been taken
down for something more important!'

There's *no* shared care here, *no* shared work. Some prison officers develop
helpful relationships with inmates and some are very interested in welfare
work, but when we entrust them with a task they seem to take for ever
getting it done. You see, they might warm to the idea of helping one day,
then the next they're out on escort duty, then they have a rest day, next
they're working a different shift. So although they might want to help, they
can't because they don't see the inmate for a few days. Already we've had
complaints from people coming in to do 'Pre-Release' because the officers
haven't been available to escort inmates to them.

(Probation officer, women's prison, June 1988)

Complaints about lack of central direction and lack of co-ordination of activities
between different parts of systems are common to many organizations and are not
peculiar to prisons. There are, however, two dimensions of prison organizations
that are distinct: the escort duty which lays on the governor the responsibility for
producing prisoners at court and which results in her inability to know from day to
day how many officers she will have available for duties in the prison; and the
unpredictability of the timing of parole board decisions concerning a prisoner's
release on parole, which makes it difficult both to plan prisoners' pre-release
programmes and to arrange for their accommodation and employment after they
have left prison. While these two factors continue to subvert the organization of
education classes and the forward planning of individual prisoners' pre-release
programmes, many people within the prisons, i.e. those who are actually responsible for operationalizing the Prison Department's schemes and programmes, will
remain sceptical about the Department's will to limit the damage that prison does.
Escort duty to and from the courts does not *have* to be done by prison officers – a
separate prison/court escort service could be established; and the parole board *could*
liaise much more with the prisons. Less amenable to change, however, are those
penal ideologies (and resultant penal regimes) which both contradict the liberal
rhetoric and subvert the aims of the new education and pre-release packages. These
ideologies are central to the effective meanings of women's imprisonment.

Penal ideologies which subvert education and pre-release schemes in the women's prisons

1 Numbers game

The most frequently expressed (and therefore most explicit) common-sense explanations for any inadequacies in education or other provision for women prisoners are rooted in arguments that because there are relatively few women prisoners it would be uneconomical to provide the range of facilities available to male prisoners. In fact, if, as I suggest in the final chapter of this book, the women's prison population were to be drastically reduced and a non-punitive ethos to be engendered within the prison guards of those few still imprisoned, an effective range of facilities *could* be provided.

2 Prisons are for punishment

The punitive regimes in women's prisons have been described in detail elsewhere. (See Carlen, 1983a – in part an analysis of the Scottish women's prison but one which is, unfortunately, still applicable to women's imprisonment in England. See also McShane, 1980; O'Dwyer and Carlen, 1985; Peckham, 1985; Mandaraka-Sheppard, 1986; GLC Women's Committee, 1986; Bardsley, 1987; Padell and Stevenson, 1988; Carlen, 1988).

The notion that, in addition to deprivation of liberty, imprisonment should impose punishment through the nature of the prison regimes themselves is evident in the way that education, accommodation in a mother and baby unit, and recreational activities are seen as privileges rather than as rights. Even when prisoners are housed in the hospital wing it is often stressed that 'they don't get away with anything just because they're here' (nurse in prison), while an oft-voiced fear of prison officers is that when outside groups (or researchers) go into the gaols women attending their sessions 'get coffee and biscuits [or cigarettes] that the others don't get' (prison officer).

If prisoners are to make the best use of their time in prison it is important that their access to health, welfare and educational opportunities is not obstructed by prison officers' still strong adherence to the principles of (a) less eligibility, i.e. that prisoners should not be better off in prison than they would have been outside; and (b) deterrence through punishment, i.e. that, if prisons are sufficiently punitive, offenders will be deterred from committing further crime (cf. Downes, 1988:68). With an overall reconviction rate of between 34 and 41 per cent for females discharged between 1980 and 1984, we have statistical evidence that in the early 1980s a custodial sentence did not deter over a third (at least) of all women imprisoned (Home Office, 1987:114), while since then we have had abundant testimony from other sources that even when women do not re-offend, the effects of the punitive prison regimes impede rather than facilitate their rehabilitation (see O'Dwyer and Carlen, 1985; Peckham, 1985; O'Dwyer *et al.*, 1987).

3 Being 'realistic'

An ideology which directly competes with the aim of equipping prisoners to lead a 'better life' upon release than that which they had led prior to imprisonment is the 'realism' which asserts that most prisoners (a) do not want to change, (b) should not be educated above their station and (c) should not be led to believe that life either can or will be better upon release. Listen:

Some women don't want a job. Like one who had four kids; the dole [sic] money was so good she didn't want a job.

(Teacher in a women's prison, 1988)

We mustn't overeducate people in prison. It's no use a woman doing an Open University degree if she's going back on the streets.

(Female official in Prison Department, 1988)

We must make women realistic about their chances. Make them realize they'll most likely be unemployed and won't get a flat just like that, just because they've been in prison.

(Prison officer, women's prison, 1988)

Whilst the specially equipped home economics room was ideal for teaching purposes, it might nonetheless be regarded as somewhat unrealistic in relation to the conditions which many inmates would face on their release or discharge.

(Home Office, 1985b – about Askham Grange)

If the foregoing views were to gain an ascendancy in prison circles it is difficult to see how any education or pre-release courses would run at all – except for prisoners who did not really need them!

4 'The main concerns of women prior to release are about personal relationships'

The belief that women are essentially creatures living primarily according to their emotions and dependent upon personal relationships to give meaning to their lives is an ideology which has not only been responsible for the dependency-inducing domesticity inherent in penal regimes and prison education for women (see Carlen, 1983a; Dobash et al., 1986), it has also increased that dependency by not taking women's employment needs seriously. The 1987–9 WPRC Biennial Report sums up the situation well, a situation underlined in January 1989 when Prison Department officials stressed to me that employment was NOT a major pre-release concern of female prisoners. WPRC explains why:

For women in prison there is little emphasis on getting a job, whereas in men's prisons employment and training are given higher priority. Women are often not considered to be breadwinners in their own right.

(WPRC, 1989a)

Of course, such a traditional view of women's role is also reinforced by the ideology of 'realism' about unemployment generally, a 'realism' which induced a speaker at a SACRO (Scottish Association for the Care and Rehabilitation of Offenders) meeting I attended in 1981 to claim that, given the increasing numbers of people out of work, prisoners should in future be educated for *un*employment rather than employment. The deleterious effects on prisoners of this 'realism' is, in the case of women, further boosted by prevailing Conservative Party ideology concerning the importance of so-called 'family values' (see Carlen, 1988). I do not, of course, question the truth of assertions that many women *are* very concerned about the deterioration of personal relationships while they are in prison. But a proper concern about family and personal relationships on the part of women should not debar them from receiving the same employment training as men. While women continue not to receive sufficient training, encouragement and support to 'go it alone' upon release, the ideology that 'women are more con-cerned about personal relationships' becomes a self-fulfilling prophecy; ill-equipped to provide for themselves, they have to go back to an unsatisfying (or even downright destructive) relationship in order to get a roof over their heads or, maybe, just a bed for the night.

Post-release conditions which work against fulfilment of the aims of prison education and pre-release schemes

Without wishing to detract from the praiseworthiness of the Prison Department's current attempts to modernize the education programmes in women's prisons and develop effective pre-release schemes in *all* gaols, it has to be noted in any assess-ment of the likely effects of these new pre-release packages that, concurrent with the regime innovations *within* penal establishments, government cuts affecting welfare, housing, education and health provision have diminished the chances of released prisoners being able to resolve the problems that may have played some part in their law-breaking and/or imprisonment in the first place (see Chapters 1, 3 and 4).

In 1981 NACRO published *Bridging The Gap: The Report of a Working Party on the Transition from Education in Penal Establishments to Education in the Community* (NACRO, 1981), which put forward a very comprehensive list of proposals for bridging the gap between prison and post-prison education. These proposals have been implemented in piecemeal fashion only and mainly by NACRO itself (see, for example, Sim, 1981; NACRO, 1988b:10). Education officers within the prisons could usually name further and higher education establishments with which they had very good links and which were sympathetic to applications from prisoners. Other institutions were mentioned as 'just not wanting to know'. Likewise with prospective employers – who can discriminate against women ex-prisoners in more ways than one! During the research the three major dimensions of employment discrimination confronting women ex-prisoners were summarized nicely by a prison officer involved with women prisoners' pre-release training and post-prison employment.

> If they don't suffer as women ex-prisoners, then they might suffer as *black* women ex-prisoners. I know of a factory which is not against employing women ex-prisoners but has a policy of not taking *black* women.

Even when women ex-prisoners do get jobs they are more likely to be part-time and at lower rates of pay than for men doing similar jobs (Pascall, 1986). Yet, whether or not they have jobs to go to, the primary concern of most women leaving prison is with accommodation; and problems relating to housing for young people, ex-prisoners and other homeless persons have also been accentuated by recent government policies. The next two chapters, therefore, will examine some of the housing, positive support, education and work schemes presently available to women ex-prisoners. They will also demonstrate how the concurrent and competing programmes of government legislation and financial cuts constantly subvert the best attempts of the voluntary and statutory agencies to help women in trouble believe there *is* a worthwhile alternative to crime.

3
A home of her own: accommodation for women in trouble and women ex-prisoners

'Housing is the subject WPRC sees most women about.'

(WPRC, 1989a)

The major problem facing a majority of women newly released from prison is likely to relate to accommodation. And although women account for only a minority of all ex-prisoners in housing need (NACRO, 1985), they face acute problems because in the main they belong to one (or more) groups against whom there has traditionally been (and still is!) housing prejudice. These particularly disadvantaged groups are comprised of: single women, lesbian women, women without men and with children, black women, drug users, the 'rootless' and disturbed, and women with histories of violence or arson. Additionally, all women have, historically, been under-provided for as tenants and homeowners in their own right (Austerberry and Watson, 1983). Recent welfare changes (Social Security Act 1986 which came into force in April 1988) and housing legislation (Housing Act 1988) have made the housing prospects of all ex-prisoners even bleaker. This chapter, therefore, will first look at the housing problems confronting women in prison; second, move on to a consideration of the range and type of accommodation available to women ex-prisoners; third, describe and discuss some of the better hostels and housing schemes designed to help women released from prison; and finally, describe and discuss the ideologies (and related policies) which result in the housing provision for women ex-prisoners being so unsatisfactory.

Housing problems of women in prison

The housing problems of women recidivists are often a cause (as well as a consequence) of at least some of their terms of imprisonment, not only in the sense that homeless offenders have a much higher reconviction rate than not-homeless offenders (see Banks and Fairhead, 1976) but also because their homelessness is too often a salient factor in the court's decision either to remand them in custody (Casale, 1989:35) or to sentence them to imprisonment (Carlen, 1983a).

Those who do have accommodation when they are sent to gaol may entertain many well-grounded fears about their flats or houses while serving time. Amongst them will be worries that: they will lose their tenancies; their homes will be squatted and/or vandalized; heating and service bills will be run up; they will lose the roof over their heads as the result of the breakup of a relationship; and owner-occupied houses will be repossessed as the result of non-payment of a mortgage. (In fact 'prisoners on remand and sentenced prisoners who will not be in prison for more than 12 months can apply for housing benefit to cover their rent and 80% of rates while they are in custody' (Green, Firth and Chandler, 1988). But women prisoners are often at a loss as to how to claim, and have in the past found it difficult to get advice. The WPRC Reception Pack (WPRC, 1989b) contains a very useful leaflet explaining what prisoners should do about their rent, etc. when they first go into prison and this, together with a hoped-for wider availability of Housing Benefit Claim forms within the prisons (see WPRC, 1989a), could lessen some of prisoners' housing worries in the future. Aggravating women prisoners' housing anxieties are the Catch 22 situations wherein (1) they will be subject to parole board demands that they get secure accommodation before they are paroled, at the same time as hostels require them to get a parole date before reserving a place; and (2) they are told by local authority social service departments that they must get accommodation before they can have their children out of Care and by local authority housing departments that they are not eligible for priority housing while the children *are* in Care. Women who have lived in a series of institutions around the country may find it difficult to find a local authority prepared to allow that they have a 'local connection' and therefore a claim to long-term housing provision from that authority. This latter situation is most likely to arise if the woman has gone straight into custody after being in local authority residential Care for several years, or if she is an older woman caught up in the revolving-door syndrome of repeated and alternating short-term stays in mental hospitals, common-lodging houses and prisons.

Even when about-to-be-released women's chances of getting a hostel place might be high, many are not prepared to apply for one unless they have already had opportunity to meet the hostel staff. Some fear that *all* hostels are authoritarian institutions little better than the prison itself. Others, known already to every hostel in their home area, correctly assume that because of previous bad behaviour they will not get a warm welcome from any hostel. Women whose children are in Care, on the other hand, often have a different concern. They fear that if they go into a hostel – even for a short time – it will be seen as evidence that they are not seriously seeking long-term accommodation for themselves and their children and that, concomitantly, they do not really want their children back to live with them. Given the present dearth of low-price housing on the market, the chances of most women ex-prisoners ever buying a home of, and on, their own are very remote indeed.

When I asked probation officers in the prisons about women ex-prisoners'

accommodation prospects they all said that outside London very little accommodation at all is available for ex-prisoners. All mentioned arsonists and drug offenders as
the two categories of ex-prisoner against whom there is most prejudice; and
'women with children' were singled out as the status-category likely to find
greatest difficulty in finding secure long-term accommodation. They themselves,
they said, confronted a variety of impediments to arranging accommodation for
women before release, the major ones being: (1) parole board delay in giving a
release date; (2) the reluctance of many hostels to reserve a room – even when a
parole date has been given; (3) the refusal of some governors to allow some
prisoners to visit hostels prior to release; (4) the prejudice of some prisoners against
all hostels which they tend to characterize as being heavily rule-governed and
authoritarian; and (5) the lack of communication between hostel and prison concerning changes in the 'places vacant' situation of specific hostels. However, some
hostel wardens were especially mentioned as being willing to visit prisons in order
to meet applicants for residence at their hostels, and WPRC workers were also
cited as being good examples of the links that are desperately needed between
hostel and about-to-be-released prisoner if a suitable match is to be made between
a woman's needs and the accommodation to be provided. Arson, it was pointed
out, is a good example of a crime where popular prejudice against those convicted
of it is based on ignorance of its possible legal meaning. For although it is generally
(and in many cases correctly) thought that an arsonist is someone who *deliberately*
sets light to property, the general public tends to be less aware of the fact that a
person can also be convicted of arson for 'endangering life' by setting fire to
something *accidentally*, e.g. by dropping a match or lighted cigarette-end when
drunk. Most hostel wardens are aware of this, and, as a result, several to whom I
spoke said they would not reject an arsonist out of hand but would want to know
about the background to the offence. Requirements like that, however, do mean
that hostels need to have very good liaison with the prisons, and it is in the cases of
very difficult-to-place prisoners like arsonists that effective links between hostel
personnel, prison staff and prisoner are essential.

Range and type of accommodation available to homeless women before the courts or newly released from prison

It was my original intention to compare the housing situation of women offenders
in Birmingham, Manchester and Stoke-on-Trent. However, even though each
area had specialist services for homeless offenders, numerical comparison of actual
hostel places available to women was not possible because of, first, my limited
resources and, second, the definitional problems surrounding the term 'housing
available to women offenders'. At one extreme, informants in probation would tell
me that accommodation for women clients could always be found and that the
women's hostels (probation-run and others) were always under-used; at the other
extreme (and more frequently) I would be told there was no chance of getting

decent accommodation at all for the majority of homeless women offenders. In between these extremes, informants ruminated at length upon the following: the type of housing which could reasonably be expected to help diminish rather than aggravate the problems of women already in trouble; the exclusions policies of the majority of hostels which, in mainly excluding those with drugs, drink and psychiatric problems (as well as those with children, physical disabilities, histories of violence or convictions for arson), manage to exclude those most in need (see for example Table 3:1); and the resultant loss of women's hostel places on the grounds of the under-utilization of existing provision.

The major providers of accommodation for ex-offenders are: NACRO who in 1987–8 had 588 places available with 990 residents during the year, 38 per cent of whom were female (NACRO, 1988b:9); and the Stonham Housing Association (not solely for ex-offenders) with over 2,350 people living in their accommodation 'some permanently, others temporarily while they are helped to secure a permanent home' (Stonham Housing Association, 1988; separate figures for females not given). Other provision is made by a number of smaller organizations all within the voluntary sector. From 1989 the Home Office is attempting to develop a national policy on after-care offender accommodation, a policy to be co-ordinated by the probation service (Home Office, 1988f). In the meantime the voluntary sector hostel accommodation available to homeless women in trouble ranges from (at best) a single room in a hostel with 24 hour support and staffing, through minimal support hostels (which are understandably quite choosy about whom they will admit) to very basic night shelter accommodation – as an emergency measure – or longer stay hostels also with very basic accommodation but willing to take women whom all other hostels reject. Reports on private hostels and accommodation were mixed, the probation officers I spoke to being, in the main, wary of the private sector, though one or two had made good contacts with private landladies offering 'satisfactory-to-superior' bedsits. (My own visit to an ex-offender in a Central London privately run block mainly tenanted to 'homeless people' in 1986 taught me that a room measuring not more than 10 feet by 10 feet and up five flights of stairs could cost £90 per week to rent.) Women with children or young women seen to be 'vulnerable' *may* qualify for council provision, but even if accepted as being in the 'priority need' category, they may still have to stay in temporary accommodation (e.g. bed and breakfast hotels or 'short life' property) for several months and, in some cases, years before they are rehoused in permanent accommodation (Green, Firth and Chandler, 1988). As for probation-run accommodation, in 1988 there were three probation/bail hostels for women-only, providing a total of 46 places; 1 bail hostel for women (and children) providing 12 places; 25 probation/bail hostels for men and women totalling 507 places; 4 bail hostels for men and women providing 64 places; 5 probation/bail hostels providing sheltered work for 109 men; one probation/bail hostel providing sheltered work for 30 men and women; and 62 probation/bail or bail-only hostels with over 1,000 places for men-only (NAPO, 1988).

Table 3:1 Ten hostels specifically for ex-offenders in London, showing range of exclusions

Hostel No.*	Sex	Exclusions
1 (Stockdale House)	Women	None initially
2	Mixed	Current alcohol, drug and mental health problems, physical disabilities
3	Mixed	Arsonists
4	Mixed	Drugs, arson, violence (treated with caution)
5	Mixed	Current drug, alcohol problems; mental ill health; violence against women and racist attacks
6	Mixed	Current drugs, alcohol and psychiatric problems
7	Women	Physicially dependent on alcohol and drugs
8	Mixed	Drugs, alcohol, psychiatric problems; arsonists, record of violence
9	Mixed	Drugs or drink problems; arsonists
10	Mixed	Arsonists, sex offenders

* Hostels are referred to by number not name as the purpose of listing their exclusions is not to criticize them but merely to show how such exclusions are likely to affect ex-offenders and ex-prisoners.

Overall then, the accommodation that might be available to homeless women in trouble or about to be released from prison can be divided into six major categories: night shelters for people needing emergency short-stay accommodation; open access hostels for older women with severe problems and younger women needing short-stay accommodation; up-market hostels with low support, i.e. for women who are without drink, drug or psychiatric problems and have no histories of violence or convictions for arson; specialist up-market hostels for women with particular problems; bail hostels and up-market hostels specifically for ex-offenders; and local authority short-stay or more permanent housing for women qualifying for council provision. Each type of hostel for women-only has its 'mixed' counterpart but, as when women talked about the problems of 'mixed' hostels they lumped them all together so that they were subsumed by their 'mixedness', I shall discuss 'mixed' hostels separately when I assess below the contribution that each kind of provision makes (or does not make) to the varied housing needs of women in trouble or newly released from prison. In assessing that contribution it is necessary to bear in mind the concept of 'accommodation viability'.

Accommodation viability

Although in the early stages of this research I had pored over many accommodation and hostel directories, I soon realized that as far as women offenders in need of accommodation are concerned, the significant question concerns the viability of the accommodation (as formally described) for individual would-be applicants. Thus 'hostel for males and females' often means that one or two women can occasionally find vacancies in a hostel run primarily for men. Hostels 'for ex-offenders' often exclude so many types of offence-category that the few women who do qualify for admission are able to get accommodation elsewhere anyhow. Other 'accommodation available', though it might have vacancies suited to the needs of an about-to-be-released prisoner, is often too far away from the area where the woman has friends or relatives; for example, the only three women-only probation/bail hostels are in Birmingham, Liverpool and Worcester – with a bail-only hostel in London. Finally, some accommodation, though it might look 'ideal' on paper, is just not viable in terms of the unrealistic expectations its staff entertain about women's rehabilitation needs. (I think in particular of the staff of a hostel in Scotland who asked my opinion as to why their newly opened hostel for women ex-prisoners was always empty. Not many applicants had actually accepted offers of residence and those who had had left within a few weeks. Not surprisingly, women just out of gaol had not taken to a regime involving compulsory programmes of daily advice sessions, supervised outings, curfews and no visitors – including children!)

Mixed hostels

As I have suggested above, many so-called 'mixed' hostels are not viable accommodation as far as women ex-offenders are concerned, and primarily for three reasons. First, many women coming out of prison or in trouble have been so abused by men that they are scared of living under the same roof as males. Second, a number of women ex-prisoners, though not scared of men physically, feel they do not wish to risk involvement in a sexual relationship until they have other areas of their lives sorted out. (Men are often hostile to mixed hostels for the same reason.) Third, in some hostels women are in such a minority that, though they would not mind a 50/50 mix, they feel oppressed by the all-male atmosphere dominating the houses. The resultant low take-up of available places can reduce still further the number of beds kept for women; places originally earmarked for females are assigned to men by staff anxious to maintain their hostel's funding by being able to show full-capacity use on their next year's grant application forms.

The woman leader of a residential project for relapsed alcoholics in Manchester gave an excellent outline of the complexities involved in attracting females to mixed projects where women are in a tiny minority. In the first 21 months of its existence the project had housed 8 women and over 70 men.

> I would have liked this hostel to have had more women but if we had waited [kept beds] for more women we would have been closed down. For whatever reason, women with drink problems remain less visible and women with commitments – like home and children – don't feel they can just go off to get treatment. They're very guilty, very secretive and much of their drinking is at home. They are much more likely to prefer to get help by going to a women's group [see Chapter 4] than by going into a hostel. There's no stigma attached to a women's group and they don't publicly have to admit to a problem. One hostel *was* intended just for women and the woman in charge worked very hard but there were just not enough women going there. They had to take men to make it financially viable. Three long-stay hostels *will* take women but they are dominated by men. Women don't want to move miles away from the area they know just to go into a women-only hostel.
>
> It's very difficult here for one woman on her own. We had to remove one woman very quickly and get her into crisis accommodation because she was being very honest with the men about her fears about rape, and unfortunately the men we had here then played on this and took the line that rape was something men *had* to do and they terrified her. You see, we tell all residents that if they're worried at night not to stay alone with their fears but to knock another resident up. But a woman in an otherwise male house can't do that. Many women do not feel that a mixed hostel is safe, and unless they have a safe place to go they're going to fall apart.
>
> (Female project leader, Mixed Alcohol Recovery Hostel, Manchester)

At a 'mixed' night shelter in Stoke-on-Trent with 26 places only 14 of 163 people staying there from January 1987 to December 1987 had been women. A female member of staff explained the disparity. 'It's a very male environment so women are not attracted.' And although a male warden of another 'mixed' hostel in Stoke-on-Trent had a paternalistic attitude towards women, he seemed to assess their presence in the hostel purely in terms of the *men's* needs.

> This unit has 16 beds maximum including 4 beds for women – which are never full. In some ways it's good to have women because it can lead to the men cleaning themselves up. But young lasses can make things difficult. They fall in with one group then fall out and go in with another group. I always explain to them, 'You may be only one woman among 12 or 13 men', and

then it's up to them. But I warn them about falling in love; I say, 'You may fall in love but then you may fall out of love'.

We keep an eye on women; they can cause trouble.

(Male warden, Stoke-on-Trent)

Need more be said?

Night shelters

Night shelters provide emergency accommodation for people with little or no money, though 'staying in a Department of Health and Social Security Resettlement Unit constitutes a claim for supplementary benefit, and charges made by voluntary night shelters are usually met by benefits to which the user is entitled' (Yapp, 1987:6). Accommodation is in dormitories or shared rooms and users can either be referred by other agencies or queue up on a 'first come first served' basis. Staff usually interview users to find out whether they are suitable for referral to longer term accommodation and in theory they are prepared to take anyone in need of shelter for the night. In practice most night shelters operate a banned list of people who have caused trouble during previous stays, and Yapp (1987) found also that among residents there could be high levels of discrimination against black people, lesbians and gay men. When homeless and isolated women leaving prison refuse help with accommodation because they do not wish to go to a more up-market hostel which they think will have too many onerous rules, it is likely that they will either sleep rough or go to a night shelter for a few nights. Likewise with youngsters who leave home because of disputes with their parents, and any other poverty-stricken persons suddenly bereft of accommodation and with nowhere to go. Yet for people already in trouble, night shelters are often frightening and abhorrent. Young people can be sickened by the sight of older people with drinking and drugs problems; there is a general fear of violence; and with a population of residents who have been walking the streets all day, tension can be high. Night-shelter staff can be successful in referring some people to more permanent accommodation, and for youngsters adrift in the metropolis and other large conurbations the night shelter can be a first point of contact with specialist agencies equipped to give them more enduring support. However, in her study of emergency night shelters in Central and Inner London, Yapp found that the existence of emergency night shelters was not widely known to young people in need, but that once they had experienced them many did not stay long enough to be referred to something better.

The process of securing a bed in an emergency night shelter is seldom simple. The shelters are not widely publicised to young people and many non-specialist agencies know little about them. A young person, who becomes homeless for the first time, may well pass through, for example, the local authority housing department, social services, the Samaritans, and a voluntary advice agency before finding a place to stay just for that night. This involves

48 Alternatives to Women's Imprisonment

finding each agency, waiting to be seen and explaining the situation to each in turn. It probably also means walking half way across London for a bed that will be waiting for them if no one turns up first. . . . Young people felt night shelters were at least better than sleeping rough, although the shelters themselves all had experience of young people leaving because of the conditions they found themselves in.

(Yapp, 1987:14, 19)

Open-access hostels

In distinguishing between emergency night shelters and open-access hostels I am making a distinction between emergency accommodation catering for people who, it is assumed, will move on after a few weeks, and those open-access hostels willing to accept (a) people making little attempt to find other accommodation; (b) people unlikely to get better or more permanent accommodation; and (c) people banned from other hostels. This is not to deny that open-access hostels do attempt to resettle people but it is to recognize that they are willing to take people that 'some hostels wouldn't touch with a barge pole' (hostel staff worker). It also means that these hostels have a high proportion of people who are disturbed or who have previously been in mental hospitals. Older residents often stay for many years.

There is rarely an age limit in the large hostels although most residents are middle-aged or older. There are few options for older single women who become homeless, whereas staff often suggest alternatives for young women . . . Younger women who stay long in these hostels tend to have come from other institutions, such as mental hospitals, and some have been brought up in children's homes. Older women cross a broader spectrum. Some are alcoholics, or have been diagnosed as chronically mentally ill. Others, including many over retirement age, have no problems beyond their homelessness.

(Austerberry and Watson, 1983)

These hostels will accept women discharged from prison but, given that homelessness is the only common denominator amongst women in open-access hostels, they are attractive neither to those who wish to make a fresh start in supportive surroundings nor to those wishing to regain their independence after months in prison – and maybe years in residential care before that.

There are many stringent conditions in these hostels. Some are designed to curb the anti-social or self-destructive behaviour of a minority of residents, like the no-drink rule to prevent violence amongst heavy drinkers. In some hostels bathroom doors could not be locked in case women drowned themselves in the bath. These rules mean, however, that everyone is living at the lowest common denominator.

(ibid.:19)

Yet for some women 'home' *is* an open-access hostel. Two women-only hostels I visited in Greek Street, Soho, London exemplified both the better type of provision which can be made for very difficult-to-place women as well as the restrictions made necessary by the severe personal difficulties of some of the residents who, none the less, view 'their' hostel as a permanent home.

The House of St Barnabas at 1 Greek Street admits women aged 17 to mid-70s and will take any women except those currently having drink and drugs problems, women on bail or arsonists. Many of the long-term residents have psychiatric problems. By day there is 14 hour cover. Provision is made for the infirm (invalid bath/shower and WC), and although the accommodation is in dormitories with curtained cubicles there is a great deal of support for individuals. Pregnant women can be housed (again, in dormitories) but those needing special medical care cannot be looked after. A staff member gave me a very full description of the House, its rules and its residents when I visited in 1988.

People come and go from here very quickly. Some move to other hostels, some just drift off, some work and save to live somewhere (but that's very rare). We don't throw many out. If they're not signing-on [for benefits] we have to ask them to go.

A large percentage of women here have psychiatric problems – but they don't cause problems for other residents. People who're drinking can't stay, and we can't cope with drugs but if they *say* they want to come off drugs we'll take them. Arsonists can't really be taken because it's such an old building and there's a fire risk. Most of the women we take from prison have committed crimes like robbery, assault, burglary.

A couple of times we've had to call the police – for violence and abuse – but it's very rare that we have to call them. They come if we've got a problem and they refer women who need a bed.

This is a *home*, so we have as few rules as possible but they have to be in by 11 during the week and 11.30 on Saturday. During the day they can stay in all the time. Some go out to day centres. There is no privacy here but there are many common rooms, two TV rooms and a quiet room. They can have visitors in the TV room.

An inter-agency group provides a lot of support. Two doctors are paid a nominal fee for seeing our women, we can call a psychiatric nurse and we have good links with social workers.

The kind of people who come here include runaways, people from prison, very well educated people – anyone who has been abandoned. The majority of young women have been in residential care. Many women have been physically or sexually abused by families or foster families. It would be nice to get more help for them. It's not just younger women who suffer from these problems, older ones do too. We sometimes get people rehoused. Recently we had one woman rehoused in Mayfair. Now she comes back two or three times a week and does her washing here. That's the best way to rehabilitate women – move them on to independence and then let them come back to the place and people when they want to. But it would be a big fib to tell you that homeless women stand a good chance of getting accommodation.

(Female hostel staff-worker, House of St Barnabas, London)

'59 Greek Street, opposite', said my informant at the House of St Barnabas, 'will often take women that we can't take', and the hostel workers at 59 Greek Street confirmed that.

We take women that no other hostel would entertain. We take arsonists, alcoholics and drug takers. But they mustn't be violent or racist. Also if they won't claim from the DHSS they have to go. We try to take older women – the ones here already are quite old – but we can't take anyone who can't manage stairs. We sometimes have to refuse over-60s and disabled people because of the nature of the building but if they can cope they can stay. We can't be a bail hostel either because we can't be held responsible.

(Hostel worker, 59 Greek St, London)

The 24 hour cover at 59 Greek Street means that women can be accommodated who are not considered to be safe risks at other hostels lacking such cover, and even women whose behaviour results in them being banned are readmitted after a month. Self-referrals are allowed to book in without interview, and only minimal counselling is provided – upon request. However, the very nature of the women's difficulties and behaviour patterns does result in 59 Greek Street being, on the one hand, a haven for the women that nobody else wants (see Carlen, 1983a) and, on the other, a place which is avoided by women (with or without problems) wanting peace, quiet, privacy and a stable environment.

The House of St Barnabas and 59 Greek Street well illustrate how hostel policies are determined by an interplay of management intent, buildings and amenities, staffing and financial resources, the behaviour of the residents themselves and the type of exclusions policy in operation. For in being tolerant of women excluded from other hostels the most tolerant hostels effectively exclude women wanting a more ordered existence. This is not to argue against hostels like the two in Greek Street – they fulfil a desperate need – but it does highlight both the many different degrees of tolerance that are required by the relatively thin spread of women-only hostels and the difficulties of locating hostels to fit the very differing and complex needs of homeless women. As far as homeless women alone or in trouble are concerned, women-only open-access hostels can play an important part in keeping them safe from molestation or sexual exploitation. Otherwise they are usually so circumstanced that by definition they cannot provide the standard of living most people in Britain (including women in trouble and just out of prison) would ordinarily consider conducive to a better way of life.

Up-market hostels with low support

I did not visit any low-support hostels (run mainly by the YWCA, commercial enterprises and voluntary organizations) primarily because they are intended for women assumed to be fully independent and with few problems. However, I have known ex-prisoners to be accommodated in such hostels and those who have lived in them have appreciated the 'low support', welcoming it as 'non-interference'. At the same time, they have been critical of regulations not allowing them to have visitors. Not many low-support hostels assist hostellers to obtain more permanent housing, and most are for single women without children.

Specialist up-market hostels for women with particular problems

Specialist hostels cater for a specific type of person. They limit their clientele to, for example, drug users; people with alcohol problems; mothers, babies and pregnant women; people with psychiatric problems; people who are HIV positive; and homeless black people. (As can be seen from the foregoing list, specialist hostels cater broadly for two types of person, i.e. those with addictions and those (like mothers with children, pregnant women, HIV positive patients, psychiatric patients and homeless black people) who, when seeking housing, are often victims of specific forms of prejudice based on fear, ignorance or racism.) In relation to the extent of the contribution of specialist hostels to increasing the housing available to women in trouble and ex-prisoners, one of their main drawbacks is that they *are* specialist! Women who might qualify on the grounds of their addiction might also have children, suffer from psychiatric problems or need support for a problem quite unconnected with the one qualifying them for residence in the specialist hostel. Thus, for example, a hostel for mothers, babies and pregnant women in North Staffordshire can take women from prison ('though we can't reserve a bed') but has to exclude child abusers, women with convictions for arson or violence as well as current drug abusers. A hostel in North London for 'women at risk', i.e. primarily prostitutes and victims of rape and incest, 'can take other women at risk but not girls with a history of alcoholism, drug abuse, schizophrenia, or arsonists' (project leader)! As far as drug rehabilitation units are concerned: many of them will not take women straight from prison; all want a commitment from in-going residents to abandoning the addiction (a commitment that many women leaving prison feel unable to make); a majority have no provision for mothers with children; and most – like other specialist hostels – put limits on visitors during the day and absolutely prohibit them from staying overnight. Such rules, though reasonable in providing protection, privacy and space to other hostellers, limit the scope for individual women to entertain their friends and satisfy sexual needs.

Bail hostels and up-market hostels specifically for women ex-offenders

During the research period I visited Kelley House, a bail hostel in London; Crowley House, a women-only probation hostel in Birmingham; Longden House, a NACRO women's hostel in Manchester; Stockdale House, a Griffins Society hostel for women ex-offenders in North London; and also a mixed probation hostel, Katherine Price-Hughes House in London. There was no women-only hostel for ex-prisoners or women in trouble in Staffordshire, though a short-term mother and baby hostel in Newcastle-under-Lyme was prepared to accept women who had been in prison – so long as they met other criteria, i.e. had a child/ children or were pregnant and were not drug takers, drinkers or arsonists. Although each of the hostels specifically for offenders and ex-offenders was slightly different to the others, they all seemed to be characterized by a greater flexibility than other hostels, a well thought-out staff position concerning the hostel's aims and ethos, a supportive structure and a willingness to reserve beds for about-to-be-released prisoners.

Kelley House Approved Bail Hostel, London
A national resource administered by the Griffins Society

Kelley House takes women who would otherwise be remanded in custody. No category of offence or offender is excluded though anyone likely to present a risk to the safety of other hostellers, staff or themselves are unlikely to be accepted. But women who have only just stopped using heroin can be accepted as a high level of support is offered by a visiting medical officer and a local psychiatrist. The residents can stay indoors all day, they do not have to find work and there is accommodation for two women with babies. There is an 11 p.m. curfew but after hostellers have kept the bail conditions for a month they can apply for bail variance so that they can go away for a weekend. The staff report to the police any bailee who stays out overnight but are often prepared to reaccept them if the police agree. Visitors are allowed in the common room between 2 p.m. and 5 p.m. and arrangements can be made for special visitors to stay longer. At the time of my visit in 1988 nomination rights to council housing and housing association properties had been negotiated.

Crowley House, Birmingham
A national resource managed by West Midlands Probation

This has been a probation hostel since 1977. The stay is 12 months. A woman could be remanded here for 5 months prior to her trial but 12 months is the condition of residence. In the last 8–10 months we have been 85 per cent full. We are becoming better known in certain parts of the country and officers are becoming more aware of women's issues and we are at last not *expecting* women to go to prison, whereas before, in certain cases, they had thought imprisonment to be inevitable.

We can take 13 adults + their children. We have good local contacts and when they leave here women get their own accommodation. To keep in contact with them when they leave we bring them back to the day centre in the minibus. [See Chapter 4.]

All the rules here are directed at creating a reasonable environment. We have House Meetings at least once a week and any residents can call a House Meeting at any time. There is peer group control and more often than not we have to prevent them imposing too many rules. For instance, they wanted to ban smoking altogether in the bedrooms. They *have* made one of the TV rooms non-smoking.

We take people on an individual basis. We have to be careful with people with addictions or people convicted of arson. We would also exclude a pregnant woman if we know that her child is to be taken from her by Social Services at birth. It is too traumatic for a woman to be here with other people's children – hearing them crying at night – and not having her own with her. We always check with Social Services if such a case is likely to arise.

We haven't any facilities for disabled people but we have taken a deaf and dumb woman and a woman in a wheelchair. It is difficult for us to have some types of mentally ill women. We used to have a psychiatrist attached but he retired and now we have to rely on our GP (who, incidentally, is super) to refer women to someone.

There is 24 hour cover here but the expectation is that the member of staff on duty will go to bed.

We have an open-door policy on counselling all the time. Women and children come in and out of the office when they like – as you can see. Each woman has a key worker, but if she isn't around they know that they can share any problem with any member of staff. We also use outside counselling.

The women here are mostly those who are isolated outside. They get very few letters, have very few visitors. We also take parolees.

More of the older women tend to be on bail for drinking problems. There's a lot of cannabis round this area. We have to take people back to court if they're smoking cannabis on the premises. We took one back recently and the magistrates sent it to the High Court. The judge there took the view that it could have been dealt with by the magistrates but recognized that it was serious that the woman had cannabis here only a few days after being sentenced. But he took no action and the woman is back here now and says that she's glad we took her back. They like to know where they are but if we breach we never ask for imprisonment. Sometimes men hang around here – especially pimps. The women here like it being women only – they think that the most important thing for women is that they must be safe. When they heard that another women's hostel is to become a mixed hostel they said, 'That's not right, that's wrong. Women need to be separate from men.'

(Warden)

Longden House, Manchester
Managed by NACRO

We have places for 12 women who are referred to us through probation. A waiting list is maintained so that women can say to the parole board that they have a place. We can go to the prison to see them or they can come in here when they are on home leave. If they have a place here it helps them to get parole. We have no exclusions in principle and we wouldn't automatically turn away an arsonist. But sometimes it depends on the present composition of the house. For instance, if we had someone who was just coming off drugs we might not take someone who sold them.

We take offenders with multiple problems. They can stay here 12 months or more, it depends on how quickly they get housing. But the housing situation is getting worse – even though this local authority is better than some others. But sometimes they're offered something pretty dreadful and we won't pressurize them into taking it.

We have a waiting list but vacancies do come up and then people think we're always full so they don't try to get women in. We have good contacts with Styal prison but often prison staff don't seem to know what's available.

We can't take women with children and now other women are worried about going into their own housing – because of difficulties about the Social Fund. We get no back up for mentally ill women, no back up at all. We can't take responsibility for them but no one else will either, and they end up back in prison; it's really the biggest problem we have to deal with.

We have a minimum of rules and they're not called rules, they're called expectations. The accommodation here is bedsits and they share lounge and bathroom. Each woman has her own key, own bell and own Baby Belling cooker.

The women here prefer a single-sex hostel. When they're here it's the first time that many women have had control over their lives, the first time they're not being exploited – not to say abused – by men. Very often they haven't realized their own personal power – what they *can* do apart from men.

(Staff of Longden House, 1988)

Stockdale House, London
Managed by the Griffins Society

[Stockdale House in London has been lauded by ex-prisoners for the relaxed, supportive and tolerant atmosphere created by Warden Moira Honnan (see O'Dwyer *et al.*, 1987). In 1988 I asked Ms Honnan why it was that her hostel was seen to be so different to many others.]

There are hostels where they can't have their friends to stay, where they have to be in by midnight and where they have to go out all day. The staff nag them to get jobs. I myself have worked in an authoritarian unit and I felt that it was organized to suit the staff. I never felt that to be fair and I didn't think that you could treat women of 17+ like that.

Here, they have their own keys to the front door, they can have their friends – male and female – to stay and, when they do, the normal rules apply that apply anywhere – like not disturbing other people. This is a normal house, not a home. (Many so-called 'homes' and 'families' are just garbage.) Too many of them have been in Children's '*Homes*' where they're expected to think that these unknown adults are wonderful – and made to call them 'Uncle' and 'Auntie' – or they've been adopted or fostered and have been seen as different, and they've never had any space given to them. This is a relaxed *house* – it's only different to any other house in that all the people living here have come out of prison.

Maybe some of the women with long histories of institutionalization might prefer a more structured environment. Yet we've never had serious disruption. Once a staff member was seriously threatened but we've never had anyone hurt. People might say I am subjecting my staff to unnecessary risk by taking on all kinds of women whom nobody else will take, but what about the greater risks of confrontation in stricter regimes? These ideas could also work in a larger unit. I've worked in a unit for 70 women that was run just like this. We have so far successfully resisted pressures to refuse to take certain women, e.g. women convicted of serious drug trafficking offences, serious acts of violence or arson, or women with psychiatric histories. The place is run on a shoestring, and if I turned away the arsonists and drugs traffickers they could run it even more cheaply, because at present we have to have 24 hour a day cover.

Being a single-sex hostel, this is a safe-house for women – and most hostels are not. The staff meet the women in prison beforehand and the average length of stay is 18 months. Thirteen women can be accommodated and there's a flat for a mother and child. We rehouse people eventually.

The women here have histories of being told that they're a waste of time. No one has ever listened to what *they* want to do. The younger lesbians have often had pressure on them to be heterosexual . . . and so on.

The main problem for us is that there has never been a clear philosophy about residential places in England.

(Moira Honnan, Warden, Stockdale House, 1988)

Bed and breakfast hotels for mothers and children

If a family or individual is homeless *and qualifies* for housing from the local council . . . they are likely, in the first instance, to be placed in a bed and breakfast hotel. Most local councils have arrangements with such hotels to take in priority homeless people. Because of the acute shortage in many areas they may have to stay in this type of temporary accommodation for as long as 2–4 years.

(Green, Firth and Chandler, 1988:31)

Many ex-prisoners or rootless women who have been constantly on the move from institution to institution find it impossible to get a local authority to accept responsibility for them. Yet even if their children are not already in residential Care and a council *is* willing to accept responsibility, many are too well appraised of the conditions in bed and breakfast hotels to be prepared to wait two or three years in a bed and breakfast place until council accommodation is available. And, according to a recent report (Conway, 1988), the women's reluctance to house their children in such places is well founded. After canvassing the views of both health profession-als and mothers in bed and breakfast hotels a report by the London Food Commis-sion, the Maternity Alliance, SHAC and Shelter concluded that:

This survey is an indictment of hotel life. It shows that pregnant women, mothers and young children are living in totally unfit housing, often with little support from housing or health services, and with no idea of when they will be rehoused . . . women's and children's health is badly affected by the conditions and stresses of having to live for long periods of time in totally unsuitable circumstances. The lack of decent kitchen facilities means that most women cannot provide their families with the basic necessities of life, such as a healthy meal. The response of Central Government, local councils and health services seems to be grossly inadequate to meet their needs.

(Conway, 1988:123)

Co-ordinated/supported housing schemes

In addition to specialist hostels for homeless ex-prisoners and women in trouble, there are also some co-ordinated/supported housing schemes which not only provide accommodation but also offer previously institutionalized tenants support and practical help in moving on (and in) to independent living in self-contained flats (see Jones, 1983).

. . . supported housing is shared housing, groups of bed sitters or self-contained dwellings managed or closely supported by a social work agency, voluntary or statutory. This provision may be an entity in itself or it may be linked to a hostel or group of hostels. It is designed primarily for those in housing need as opposed to those needing residential care. . . . Supported housing projects may offer a transitional phase from institution to general housing or they may be a more permanent form of housing for those who cannot manage or do not want independent housing.

(NACRO, 1982:1)

Some of these schemes are for men only but others cater for both men and women, e.g. the Handsworth Young Person's Accommodation Committee (HYPAC) which is specifically for young black homeless people 'either going through the Birmingham law courts or being discharged from penal institutions' (HYPAC, 1985:7); and NACRO's Co-ordinated Accommodation Scheme (CAS) in London which has houses for women only, mixed houses where a specific number of beds are reserved for women, and a policy of aiming to povide 50 per cent of places to women (CAS, 1985:4).

In principle, the type of housing support and independent accommodation which co-ordinated/supported housing projects offer is ideal. Previously institutionalized young people get practical help with the intricacies of setting up and running households and also support in dealing with agencies like the DHSS which can, under certain conditions, provide the financial aid essential to furnishing and heating homes. In practice, the co-ordination of the many different agencies involved in administering the schemes has resulted in some of them operating with very stringent criteria for assessing the suitability of prospective tenants before referring them on to the next agency. For they feel that they must maintain credibility with every agency if they are to do their best for future clients. Consequently, people with serious problems other than homelessness can again be excluded. Such exclusion results not so much from a bureaucratic lack of awareness of the irony of operating a policy of exclusiveness in relation to the resettlement of already marginalized people. Rather, it is a consequence of the short supply of low-price housing to rent. Scarcity of properties to rent engenders in housing scheme co-ordinators a very real fear of losing their (usually already low) quota of nominations to housing associations of local authority accommodation.

Ideologies, practices and policies

At the beginning of this book I explained that one of its purposes was to show, by reference to existing good practice and imaginative schemes, that we already have the professional knowledge and expert experience to cut drastically the present female custodial population and keep *all* female petty offenders – together with a majority of more serious women criminals – out of prison in the future. At the same time, I argued that any crime reduction policy which was not also accompanied by effective policies to reduce poverty, unemployment and homelessness would be ineffective (see Currie, 1985; Box, 1987; and Carlen, 1988). But, throughout this book, I claimed, we would also see how the best attempts of existing rehabilitative agencies to keep female ex-prisoners out of trouble and prison are routinely subverted by sexist ideologies and government policies which narrow the legitimate options of already marginalized women still further. Nowhere can this claim be better substantiated than in relation to housing provision.

Ideologies

1 Women and family discipline

The ways in which women, instead of being seen as citizens in their own right, are represented by the courts as always-already being primarily wives, mothers or daughters either within or without nuclear family discipline have already been documented (Carlen, 1983a, 1987, 1988; Edwards, 1984; and Eaton, 1986). Dee Cook (1987, 1989) has demonstrated how female welfare claimants are similarly viewed by the Department of Social Security, while Chambers and Millar (1987) and Adler (1987) have shown that the same logic is even used to assess (and often discredit) the evidence of rape victims. It is, therefore, not surprising that the tenaciously held ideology that a woman's proper place is in the family also affects the range and administration of housing provision for women in trouble and ex-prisoners. During my research I had evidence of this in relation to the coercion of a young pregnant probationer, young women who had quarrelled with their parents and the programmes of some mother and baby hostels. A probation officer explained the circumstances under which she might have argued that prison was the best place for a young woman offender:

> One case I had recently, she had come out of Care and was homeless and rootless. We got her into a mother and baby home but if she hadn't settled there we were going to take her back to court – either a breach or because she hadn't paid her fines anyway – and we would have let her go to prison to have her baby. Yes, if she hadn't settled at the mother and baby home we would have wanted her to go to prison – for the baby's sake.
>
> (Probation officer, Staffordshire)

Another Staffordshire probation officer said that young girls who admit to having quarrelled with their parents are often told that they are to return home when they attempt to claim that they are homeless. Direct Access in Manchester and the Inner London Probation Service's Aftercare and Resettlement Office in Borough High St., London confirmed that such a policy was operated by some agencies, though they themselves tend to accept that young women claiming to be homeless are indeed homeless. None the less, when agencies *do* refuse to recognize young women's homelessness it is often the case that youngsters thus refused help allow themselves to be sexually exploited in return for a bed for the night. A probation officer at one Homeless Offenders' Unit claimed that prison staff have to bear some responsibility for the failure of some young women to get fixed up with suitable accommodation before they leave prison.

> Women in prison are pressured to put their parents' address down so that's why women's homelessness is hidden. Women are not encouraged to say they're homeless. Three out of five young girls we had recently had definitely been told to put down their parents' address. Only at the last minute had the women insisted that they were not going home to all the problems they'd had before. Quite often prison probation officers just generalize when they speak to prisoners about accommodation prospects. For instance, it's not true that they always have to go into a hostel before they get more permanent accommodation. It could stop a lot of offending if people came out to decent accommodation. I've found that those who re-offend are those who're left in limbo, with no accommodation – nothing.
>
> (Inner London Probation Service's Aftercare and Resettlement Office)

Even though women are expected to be good mothers, present Conservative Party family ideology has not resulted in better life chances for the 72,000 homeless and in priority need families with one or more dependent children (National Children's Home, 1988). A general lack of provision for homeless women with children gives the lie to the Government's claims that it is committed to strengthening family life. In some mother and baby hostels there is still a presumption that homeless mothers are feckless mothers.

We can count mother and baby hostels on one hand. Then, of them, several treat all women as if they are inadequate. Some have full programmes of childcare, nutrition, housekeeping, etc. But not all homeless ex-offenders are inadequate and I think it's very patronizing to treat them like that. All that many need is a self-contained flat with access to an office and a telephone to sort out some of their problems. So they won't consider places where people are going to be telling them what to do all the time. What they need is a *home*, not domestic science lessons.

> (Probation officer, Inner London Probation Service's Aftercare
> and Resettlement Unit)

2 *Professional ideologies concerning range and types of provision*

Professional ideologies concerning the range and types of provision for homeless women in trouble, though usually based on principles concerning the most effective forms of rehabilitation (e.g. of drug offenders), are often obstructive of the best interests of the clients whose needs the professional agencies have been set up to serve. Competition for very scarce resources has forced many hostel and co-ordinated scheme administrators into claiming that their particular project is the best and only type suitable for homeless ex-prisoners. Thus, up-market hostel staff often spoke to me with pride about their exclusiveness and good 'results' while open-access hostels spoke similarly of their tolerance of people with multiple problems − and behaviour patterns that would themselves certainly operate to exclude people of a quiet, nervous or timid disposition and with problems enough of their own! At the same time, and when pressed, all administrators agreed that there was a need for a wide range of small hostel and bedsit provision with varying degrees of support. However, a majority of respondents (including probation officers) thought that probation hostels for women were both too exclusive and too strict, a prejudice that was recognized but considered ill-founded by a woman manager in probation in Birmingham, and which I myself, having visited Crowley House, also thought might nowadays be out of date and unwarranted.

> It's always a job to get an arsonist into a probation hostel. Probation hostels are the best staffed but the most restrictive. Probation officers are not prepared to take risks. But why?
>
> (Male senior probation officer, Manchester)

> Probation hostels are not prepared to take risks. And that's ironical when you compare their [larger] salaries with mine.
>
> (Warden, Stockdale House, London)

> Probation hostels are almost impossible to get into. Women have to be on probation to get into a probation hostel and you really have to be a saint to get into one too! We here get to learn that, because we get desperate calls from

probation officers in courts who say they'll never be able to get their client into a probation hostel. But some clients won't go to a probation hostel anyhow because the regimes are too strict. With clients there's also a fear that if they don't settle into a probation hostel there'll be a comeback from probation. But probation hostels are unnecessarily strict and I'm sure if the women could be given a bit more responsibility they would react better.

(Inner London Probation Service's Aftercare and Resettlement Office)

There's under occupancy right across the board in women's accommodation. Yet probation officers often complain that it's difficult to get accommodation for women. I think this relates to three things. First, do women *want* to be moved away from their families? Because women needing hostel accommodation are more likely than men to have to move from the area where they're presently living. Second, probation officers often develop fantasies about what the hostels will accept. Third, the service tends to see women – and probation hostels – in a particular way and often referral to a probation hostel is not made. For instance, a few years ago a sixteen year old young woman stabbed and killed her lover because he'd been with another woman. While she was on bail she was found to be pregnant and a referral was made to Crowley House. She stayed there for twelve months and is now home. But when an almost identical case occurred in a neighbouring area no referral was made by the Service and the woman ended up in prison.

(ACPO, West Midlands)

Practices

When I talked with hostel and other accommodation project staff about their modes of operating, they were quick to point out that owing to adverse material and ideological circumstances beyond their control they often had to proceed in ways they knew to be less than ideal. These major circumstances beyond their control were usually cited in the following order of importance: scarcity of resources and increasing homelessness resulting from government policies; sexist, feminist and professional ideologies which often result in what little provision there is for homeless women being under-used or misused; and the apparently intractable behaviour patterns of a very few homeless women which make them unsafe or undesirable co-habitees for almost anyone else, *especially* other women under stress and striving desperately to keep on an even keel themselves. As criminal justice personnel discussed the most problematic practices relating to the administration of accommodation for women ex-offenders, these adverse material and ideological conditions surfaced again and again, and in different combinations.

1 Exclusions

One woman we had recently was a drug user *and* mentally ill. Drug places didn't want her because she was mentally ill. Hostels for the mentally ill didn't want her because she was a drug user.

(Inner London Probation Service's Aftercare and Resettlement Office)

It's a big problem – those who fall through the net one way or another. And it comes down to this: that the provision is just not there.

(Probation officer, Manchester)

Hostel exclusions policies have already been mentioned in this chapter as being constitutive of the major minefield of obstacles through which referring agencies have to pick their way when attempting to place women in a hostel or project. Yet the reasons for exclusion are not uniform but complex, and they fall into three main groups. First, there are the definitional exclusions which occur as a result of a hostel regime being specifically organized for the rehabilitation of women with a problem requiring specialist help, e.g. a drugs rehabilitation hostel will obviously only take women with a drugs problem. Second, there are the status exclusions: (1) relating to a woman's status in the criminal justice system, e.g. if she is not on bail or probation she cannot go to a bail and/or probation hostel; (2) relating to a woman's family status, e.g. if she neither is pregnant nor has children she will be excluded from a few hostels, but if she does have children she will be excluded from the majority; (3) relating to gender, e.g. as we have seen, many so-called mixed hostels prefer *not* to take women, especially attractive youngsters; (4) relating to sexual orientation, e.g. some voluntary hostels have in the past been reluctant to take lesbians; (5) relating to racism – as has already been mentioned, Yapp (1987) found that amongst the residents of night shelters there was often discrimination and racist behaviour directed at black people; and (6) relating to disability, i.e. hostel design or lack of amenity forces most hostels to exclude people who cannot manage stairs or who need specialist facilities in order to be independent. Third, there are the behavioural exclusions, directed mainly against people whose behaviour is *so* bizarre that it would usually be seen as evidence of some mental illness or abnormality, but also directed against people with convictions for arson and crimes of violence and those still abusing drugs and or alcohol.

In talking of exclusions, people working in the accommodation for ex-offenders sector thought that most problems of exclusion could be solved if sufficient resources were to be made available to provide adequately and appropriately for women with multiple personal problems, women with physical disabilities and women with children. Exclusions relating to discrimination, prejudice and racism are already being tackled by some hostels and schemes whose staff are making positive efforts to attract, for instance, black people or lesbians, or who are setting targets of 50/50 tenancies for males and females. There was also general agreement with NACRO's contention that

the housing needs of offenders are no different from those of other single homeless people. Most single homeless people need ordinary housing with access to support; only a small proportion require fully staffed hostels.

(NACRO, 1985)

The one single group of ex-offenders seen to be most difficult to provide for were those mentally ill people whose behaviour would be viewed as very disturbed (and disturbing) by most people. At the Direct Access Hostel in Manchester, a hostel committed to taking all homeless women, I saw a room that had been burnt out by a woman who had set light to it and, as the warden ruefully ruminated, there are even more complex problems to confront with mentally ill people.

> Arson *is* a problem, because 24 hour cover is very difficult. But ex-mental hospital patients can pose many other difficulties. For instance, they may be racist. Now whereas the others have the sense to keep their mouths shut even if they are racist, the mentally ill don't. We keep them here because no one else will have them. But as far as some social workers are concerned it's a dumping job; they know we'll keep them for as long as we can so they give up trying to get them anything else.
>
> (Direct Access, Manchester)

> People who are mentally ill may not be violent. They may be no trouble at all during the day, but then go round knocking other residents up at night because they are lonely. It's not very bad behaviour but it drives other residents crazy. So you can only have that kind of person if you've got 24 hour cover, so that she can talk to *you* and not disturb the others.
>
> (Staff worker, Central London hostel)

Quite reasonably, several hostels will only take mentally disturbed people on condition that social workers continue to visit, support and seek more suitable accommodation for them. None the less, because psychiatry has adopted a policy of keeping the mentally ill in the (often non-existent) 'community' (rather than in hospital) and psychiatrists have become increasingly reluctant to admit people with 'personality disorders' as hospital inmates (see Carlen, 1983a:195–211), many highly disturbed women continue to go to prison merely because there is nowhere else for them to go. Although seriously mentally disturbed women are still most likely to comprise less than a quarter of the average daily female prison population (see for instance Gibbens, 1971), until appropriate non-custodial provision is made for these most vulnerable women, any scheme of alternatives to women's imprisonment must be assessed as being grossly inadequate.

2 Categorization and referral

> All the hostels are so set on their definitions and categories.
> (Inner London Probation Service's Aftercare and Resettlement Unit)

The complex exclusions policies of the various hostels and schemes inevitably lead to equally complex assessment, categorization and referral systems which, constituted, as most of them are, within bureaucratized multi-professional agencies, further impede the delivery of an efficient service to clients. Furthermore, as so many potential clients have already suffered the coercive objectification involved in the assessment, classification and referral procedures of social services and the penal system, it is not surprising that a substantial number reject the assessing agency before it rejects them. A senior probation officer graphically described a scenario that many other referring agents had witnessed:

> The waiting time and referral procedures for some of the charities are so complicated that it takes months to get someone in. For example, I once had a most difficult and disturbed young woman and she got an interview in London for a hostel place there. She stayed two or three days at their hostel and then they turned her down. But not before she had turned them down. And she was in real need. She was being exploited by all types of seedy men and that, in the end, was what she went back to again.
>
> (Male SPO, Manchester)

Bureaucratic procedures relating to rigid categorization and delineation of task can also frustrate the work of the referral agencies themselves. An outstanding example of this relates to the work which probation homeless offenders' units do. Incredible as it may seem, and as is the case with probation-run women's groups (see Chapter 4), the work that probation homeless offenders' units do with non-statutory clients does not count as proper probation work at all!

> There's a lot of hassle about the work we do because non-statutory clients don't count in the statistics at all. So a lot of intensive, preventative work just doesn't count. But what obstacles to put in our way when we could be getting people at risk somewhere to live and keeping them out of prison!
>
> (Probation officer, Inner London Probation Service's Aftercare
> and Resettlement Unit)

It is to be hoped that when the new arrangements for a national policy on after-care for offenders come into force (Home Office, 1988f), they will be co-ordinated in such a way that most of these problems of exclusions, assessment and categoriza-tion can be ironed out. Other problems which will need addressing are: liaison and communication between schemes, hostels, statutory agencies and prisons; reserva-tion procedures for about-to-be-released prisoners together with a greater ac-countability of the parole board; and some general guidelines concerning the range of philosophies which might shape the general governance and operating modes of different types of housing provision for women.

3 Liaison and communication

A common complaint from referring agencies was that they never had up-to-date information concerning the current availability of places on schemes. From proba-tion officers there was constant criticism that sometimes homeless offender units had, in desperation, to refer clients to bed and breakfast accommodation that was decidedly inferior or even undesirable, e.g. 'being used for drugs or rent boys' (probation officer, Inner London). From the prisons the familiar cry was that hostels would not promise places to women who hadn't a release date, even though the parole board would not give them a release date until they had a promise of secure accommodation. All of these complaints could be met with more resources. In the age of advanced information technology a computerized information system could immediately supply agencies with up to the minute information concerning both availability of places and assessment criteria. With an increase in the amount of decent rented housing available, no homeless people would need to be referred to substandard or inappropriate accommodation. In a properly co-ordinated and well funded system of after-care there would be specifically designated hostels to accommodate homeless parolees.

4 'Safe houses' or independent houses for women?
Many of my informants expressed concern about the lack of a philosophy of housing for women. For, despite the fact that the referral procedures of the housing agencies are so complex, there is often a mismatch between women's needs and women's housing. Regrettably, complicated referral procedures are committed more to assessing the woman's suitability for the sought-after accommodation than to gauging the accommodation most appropriate to her needs. Two major complaints were made: on the one hand, that young women's hostels are sometimes so restrictive in relation to male visitors that youngsters are not prepared to tolerate regimes that deny opportunity for developing sexual relationships; on the other, that there are insufficient women–only hostels to accommodate those who previously have been so badly damaged (physically, emotionally and mentally) by men that they will not consider living in a mixed house. Thus, while the vast majority of complaints centred on the fact that women-only hostels are so few and far between, a male probation officer in Manchester was equally critical of hostels which refuse to recognize that, although many women want to be protected from male exploitation, others want a safe environment in which to develop non-exploitative sexual relationships with men. Yet the dilemma posed by women's contrasting needs (and principles!) in relation to the question of male visitors in women-only houses is not an intractable one. A more democratic approach to hostel management is already resulting in several hostels adapting their rules and admission procedures to suit the particular mix of women already in residence at any one time. An increase in the range and number of small supported living units would enable more women to lead their own lives in the type of housing environment of their choice. Establishment of a national forum for the assessment of women's different housing needs might ensure that in future women in trouble get the type of housing they *want* rather than that considered 'good enough' for them.

Policies

Investigation of the different types of existing housing provision for women in trouble and ex-prisoners left me in no doubt that the expertise and knowledge necessary to developing the full range of accommodation units required are already available. Recently, too, Berthould and Casey (1988) have outlined a scheme for the co-ordinated and comprehensive funding of hostels. What appears to be lacking is the political will and public funding to act on that knowledge and expertise. Since 1979–80, 'total government investment in housing construction, repair and investment has more than halved – a drop from £6,900 million to £2,600 million in 1985–6' (Shelter, 1988). The following information (taken from the Shelter Campaign Pack, 1988) highlights just a few of the results.

* London hoteliers were paid £78 million in 1987 by councils for bed and breakfast accommodation for homeless families, while the DHSS picked up a bill for £30 million.
   On average in England since 1982:
* Every week 3,670 families and single people arrive homeless at their town hall.
* There are now 23,000 homeless households placed in temporary accommodation.

With figures like these it is not surprising that women in trouble and ex-prisoners have such difficulty in finding suitable accommodation. Several of my informants expressed a faint hope that the Home Office's new scheme for co-ordinating after-care accommodation (Home Office, 1988f) might improve the situation, though others did not see how it could without a massive injection of funds into the public and charitable housing sectors. What they were more certain of was that the present local and national government policies on housing and welfare provision are likely to ensure that the housing situation of women ex-offenders gets worse in the near future. Other recent legislation (e.g. Local Government Acts 1985 and 1988) has also had implications for hostel provision for women. Furthermore, if the proposals in the Government's 1988 Green Paper, *Punishment, Custody and the Community* (Home Office, 1988c), are implemented, some hostel administrators might be tempted to tighten their regimes still further, with the likely result that women will either refuse to live in them or, if forced to reside in approved hostels as a condition of bail or a non-custodial penalty, abscond from houses which they find oppressively restrictive.

Legislation subverting attempts to provide a range of appropriate housing for women in trouble and ex-prisoners

1 Housing legislation
The 1980 Housing Act introduced the right to buy council houses and flats at a discount. Since then (and as we saw above), total government investment in public sector housing has more than halved. About 20 per cent of national public housing has been sold and, although sales have recently tailed off, some councils (e.g.

Westminster which is currently attempting to sell 9,000 vacant council properties to anyone complying with certain fairly wide criteria demonstrating a tenuous connection with the borough) are still intent on privatizing the better properties. Of those still owned by councils, 'some 85 per cent . . . require repairs and improvements – there is a backlog of around £20 billion . . . [and] the situation is continuing to deteriorate' (Audit Commission, 1986, cited in Franklin, 1988:3). Moreover, 'only 8 per cent of all housing is now being provided by landlords, compared with 32 per cent in 1960' (ibid.). Left-wing councils which, in the early 1980s, persisted in attempting to fulfil their electoral commitments to house the homeless and improve existing accommodation were 'ratecapped' (i.e. were threatened under the Rates Act 1984 with disproportionate loss of central government grant if they set rates above a government-defined limit). This was the case with Manchester City. Everywhere I went in Manchester, housing workers referred with pride to the Council's commitment to public housing and with bitterness to central government policies which constantly undermine attempts to house the homeless.

For homeless single people coming out of prison the route to decent housing has most often been via the up-market hostel, followed by the 'move-on' into an independent flat provided by either a charitable housing association or a local authority. However, because the 1988 Housing Act drastically cut the grant to housing associations, and authorized the setting up of Housing Action Trusts to take over large areas of run-down council housing with no obligations for housing the homeless, it is likely that the amount of 'move-on' accommodation will be considerably reduced. Even where offers of flats are still made to people living in homeless hostels, the increased rents that housing associations will be forced to charge will make the offers unrealistic for people subsisting on welfare benefits. If the rent *is* affordable, recent social security legislation will impede the new tenant's efforts to furnish the accommodation (see also Day, 1989).

2 Social Security Act, 1986
Changes in social security authorized by the Social Security Act 1986 were implemented in April 1988. The major changes affecting the homeless were:

1 'Urgent Needs Payments' to allow a homeless person with no money to book into cheap accommodation were abolished, and replaced with 'Crisis Loans' from the new 'Social Fund' repayable from benefits.
2 One-off and non-repayable grants for clothes, bedding and other necessities were abolished and replaced by Social Fund loans to be made at official discretion only on condition that (i) the relevant DSS office has the money available in its limited funds and (ii) claimants are assessed as being able to make the repayments.

At first, too, Income Support was paid in arrears. However, in a written answer made on Wednesday, 19 October 1988, Nicholas Scott, Secretary of State for

Social Security, indicated that the system had been modified in recognition of the needs of homeless people. Notwithstanding these modifications, horror stories abound about the systematic denial of financial help to the homeless and destitute. Two reproduced in a report by the Central London Social Security Advisers Forum (CLSSAF) illustrate some of the effects that the recent changes have had on provision for women.

Pat Rice, Welfare officer, Cecil Housing Association:

My client was staying at a hotel – she is now living at a homeless women's hostel. While she was in prison for three and a half weeks her clothes were stolen from the hotel. She applied for a Community Care Grant or a Social Fund Loan to replace it in April. The DHSS decided yesterday, 25 July, to refuse her both, the grant as she was not in prison for more than three months, and the loan because there was a break in her claim for more than 14 days while she was in prison.

We have two hostels for single homeless women, one dealt with by Bloomsbury DHSS and the other by Southwark. We had a meeting with the manager from one of the DHSS offices, who I don't really wish to identify, asking him about the changes in benefit to under 18's which are due later this year.

We are already struggling to keep the hostels going financially. We explained to him the situation where if we get an under-18 come to us with no money, while the DHSS are making their investigations we will have to put them up, and feed them of course, full board, whilst the investigations are being carried out.

I asked him, if, at the end of these investigations it is decided they are not entitled to any benefit, what is going to happen regarding our hostel deficit grant payment?

The manager of the DHSS told us that that is when our real charity begins.

Debbie Hyams, Kentish Town CAB:

A young pregnant woman was on Supplementary Benefit for some time, and is now on Income Support. She was homeless and living in bed and breakfast, placed there by the council. She was then offered a housing association tenancy.

She applied to the Social Fund for furniture money, which was refused on the grounds that she had had a break in her claim, and hadn't been continuously in receipt of benefit for 26 weeks. She had in fact got herself a temporary job for about 10 weeks leading up to Christmas, and of course that barred her from any help at all from the Social Fund.

In the end she was reduced to accepting a cooker and a bed from the housing association itself, and a few sticks of furniture that were found which would otherwise have been thrown out. She may be able to reapply when she has been in continuous receipt of benefit for six months, but by that time it will be near the birth of her child and she will have been living in the flat without furniture for some time.

(Gosling, 1988:23–4)

Informants at Inner London Probation Service's Aftercare and Resettlement Office told a similar tale.

> At present no one is getting a Crisis Loan round here. Even if they're sleeping on the street! The DHSS says they're not in crisis because if they've slept rough once and survived, then they're used to it and can do it again. The further down you get, the less you get out of them. People have given up. They think they've got to fill in so many forms, go to so many interviews and still not get anything. So they're not applying. Which is what the government wants. They'll use it to justify further cuts.

3 The Local Government Act 1985

The legislation which resulted in the demise of the Greater London Council in 1987 had the effect of reducing or abolishing the funding of a number of projects helping women in trouble. These voluntary (and often self-help) organizations were in several cases assisting women whose difficulties were so complex that they had already been denied help by all of the statutory agencies.

4 Local Government Act 1988

> Many lesbians become homeless or experience housing difficulties as a direct result of other people's hostile reaction to their sexuality. They have suffered hostility and even physical violence in temporary and shared accommodation and further discrimination and prejudice in trying to find suitable permanent housing. Some councils and organisations have begun to acknowledge and respond to the housing needs of lesbians and gay men in the face of hostility, prejudice and physical attack. They may now withdraw their services for fear of prosecution under the Local Government Act 1988 which prohibits the 'intentional promotion of homosexuality', while giving little guidance as to how this will be interpreted.

(Green, Firth and Chandler, 1988)

Punishment, custody and the community

As should have become apparent by now, the empirical research for this book on *Alternatives to Women's Imprisonment* was in full swing when, in July 1988, the Government published its Green Paper, *Punishment, Custody and the Community* (Home Office, 1988c), in which it outlined its strategy for reducing the prison population. Based on the unfounded assumption that sentencers over-impose custodial sentences because they lack faith in the non-custodials, the plan was to stiffen existing alternatives – supposedly to make them more attractive to judges and magistrates – and (maybe) introduce a few more. Since then a number of organizations and individuals have published critical (and largely hostile) responses (NAPO, 1988b; Raynor, 1988). As far as homeless women offenders are concerned we must conclude, on the evidence presented in this chapter, that it is just not feasible to expect them to suffer further punishment in the community. They are already suffering enough. Furthermore, if as a result of the Green Paper, more stringent conditions are introduced into bail and probation hostels, two of the most important existing types of non-custodial and after-care provision will effectively have been lost. More importantly, and again on the evidence presented in this chapter, we have to conclude that while new antisocial legislation affecting every area of public life continues to promote inequality, poverty and homelessness, the non-custodial sentiments of *Punishment, Custody and the Community* will not result in a reduced prison population. Moreover until criminal justice policy is subordinated to, and co-ordinated with, a strategy for social justice in general (see Carlen, 1989), we can expect homeless and destitute recidivist offenders to continue to go to gaol.

4
Women together: being, education, work

We have found a confidence which we never knew we had. We have proved to ourselves and our men that we are as strong as they are. We learnt so much in this, our struggle, and we know now that it is the same struggle as many others.

(Doreen Humber and Pauline Radford talking about the 1984 miners' strike in Britain, cited in Beaton, 1984:265)

Women need the chance to say, 'This is me. Here I am.' That is what the group does for women.

(Woman probation officer, Cardiff, 1988)

As unemployment has bitten deep into the social fabric of 1980s Britain, the major burdens of ensuing poverty have been borne by women and especially lone mothers with children (Bull and Wilding, 1983; Campbell, 1984; Pascall, 1986; Townsend *et al.*, 1987; Glendinning and Millar, 1988). It is not, therefore, surprising that 1980s research into women's imprisonment has revealed that the majority of women in prison have also suffered poverty at some time prior to their involvement in criminal activities (Mandaraka-Sheppard, 1986; Genders and Player, 1987; Carlen, 1988). Everyone I met who was running a group or hostel specifically for women offenders acknowledged that relief from poverty was the primary need of most of their (variously called) clients, members of the collective, or residents. Yet, at the same time, they were also insistent that there were other needs to be met: for example, the need to build up confidence and self-esteem; the need to acquire the skills of assertiveness; educational and training needs; and so on. Not one of my informants was fool enough to believe that membership of a women's group would diminish poverty. But project leaders and women offenders themselves recognized that if ever they were to make the most of what few opportunities might come their way in the future, they needed to be strengthened for the twin struggles of making a living *and* being law-abiding. It was in recognition of the fact that women's strength lies in women's solidarity that female ex-prisoners founded the theatre company *Clean Break* in 1978, the *Creative and Supportive Trust* (CAST) in 1981 and the campaigning and support group *Women in Prison* (WIP) in 1983 (see Carlen and Tchaikovsky, 1985). When in 1988 I undertook the postal survey of probation projects and programmes specifically designed for women, I was curious as to the extent to which probation had taken on board the reiterated claims of women ex-prisoners' support groups that the needs of women offenders and ex-prisoners are different to those of their male counterparts and that often they are best met in a women-only environment.

The survey of probation provision specifically designed for female offenders

Fifty seven probation services in England, Wales and Northern Ireland were invited to give information about the provision for women offenders in their areas and 41 replied, only 1 service refusing to give information and the other 40 providing the information as requested. Replies were not received from 16 services. (See Appendix for a list of the services from which replies were received.) Of the 40 services which did reply, 21 said that at the time of writing there were no probation-run groups specifically for women in their areas, though 9 of these indicated that they were aware of women's needs and attempted to cater for them as they arose. For several, however, the need to provide specifically for women did not arise very often, either because, like Wiltshire, they were 'a very small area' or because, like Dorset, they saw themselves as having relatively few females threatened with custody. In fact, Dorset's reply is worth quoting as I suspect it echoes the logic on which several services base their policy towards women offenders, 'There is very little actually for women within Dorset as the number of women committed to custody from Dorset for the year 1986 was 6 – immediate imprisonment – 1 – Youth Custody.' At the other end of the scale, 7 probation services could name between 4 and 9 women-only groups, with Staffordshire (9), Greater Manchester (8) and Avon (8) topping the league. The remaining 11 services ran 1 or 2 groups specifically for women. All services pointed to a range of mixed provision available to both sexes, and some services, particularly Inner London, drew attention to non-probation-run women's groups to which clients with special needs (e.g. alcohol or other drug problems) could be directed. To investigate in greater depth how 3 services – Greater Manchester, West Midlands and Staffordshire – viewed provision for women offenders and ex-prisoners, I asked the Chief Officers of each service to direct me to the probation personnel most closely involved with either women's issues or projects for women in each area.

At the time of my research in 1988 one senior probation officer (SPO) in the City of Manchester had recently been given responsibility for gender issues, and I was initially put in touch with that SPO and through her with the officers running women's groups. In the West Midlands service a number of officers had in the months immediately preceding my research become very concerned about issues pertaining to women offenders, and my initial contact, an Assistant Chief Probation Officer, was therefore able to put me in touch with several women-only probation-run groups, explaining as she did so:

We developed a higher profile on sexism after we'd started anti-racism training and awareness. We haven't got a 'gender-awareness' officer but we recently appointed an equal opportunities officer. Amongst all the women
managers in the Midlands there is a concern about women's issues. Many of
the male officers are WMCPs, to put it mildly.

(ACPO, Birmingham)

Staffordshire, in the summer of 1988, did not have an officer appointed specifically
to deal with provision for female offenders but, as there were already 9 women-
only probation-run groups in the county, the Chief Probation Officer directed me
to their leaders who indicated that there was at least as much awareness of gender
and women's issues amongst Staffordshire probation officers as there was amongst
officers of Greater Manchester and the West Midlands. Indeed, the existence of 9
flourishing women's groups suggests that perhaps Staffordshire probation officers
were among the first to act on the growing awareness of gender issues in probation.

Talking with probation officers and women's groups in Greater Manchester, the
West Midlands and Staffordshire left me with two dominant impressions: one was
of the enthusiasm of the group participants and the tremendously positive and
innovative role that women's groups have to play in the rehabilitation of women
ex-prisoners and the prevention of women's crime; the other was of the innumerable threats to their existence which women's groups face as they repeatedly
confront sexism, financial restrictions and the contemporary political prejudices
against *any* purely deterrent and non-punitive work in probation. As, however, it is
a major aim of this book to spread word of some of the more positive non-
custodial programmes for women, let us now (before analysing the barriers to their
continued existence) look at the main types of women-only probation-run groups
that existed in Greater Manchester, the West Midlands and Staffordshire in summer 1988. (In what follows I shall also be quoting from probation officers from
other areas – as will be indicated.)

Probation-run women's groups

All of the women's groups about which I received information during the course
of this research were either composed entirely of voluntary clients or a mixture of
voluntary and Schedule 11 section 4(B)s (see Criminal Justice Act 1982). This was
not surprising. Outside the large conurbations only a few women in any one area
are usually high enough up the sentencing tariff to be in danger of a custodial
penalty. Day centres run solely for the benefit of women 4(B) offenders would not,
therefore, be considered feasible in terms of either the costs involved or the
numbers likely to attend. Thus most of the women's groups met only weekly and
catered primarily for voluntary clients, with a few 4(B) clients attending as a
supplement to their attendance at a mixed centre on other days of the week.
However, the voluntary groups varied in the degree of structure which they had,

and while some concentrated solely on support and welfare activities, others, even though they were not offering a Schedule 11 4(B) programme, were anxious to be seen by the courts as serious alternatives to custody, and, in furtherance of this aim, offered programmes concentrating on offending behaviour.

The justifications for women's groups

The overall justifications for the women's groups were the same as for any other type of probation work with offenders:

1 To avert custodial sentences where appropriate.
2 To provide the courts with greater flexibility in dealing with offenders facing custody.
3 To offer the courts the option of making a Probation Order designed to exert greater elements of control and intensify the frequency and quality of probation/client contact.
4 To promote the good conduct of the offender with a view to eliminating further offences.

Additional specific justifications for having women-only groups

1 Concern about the numbers of women going into custody

In 1987 the women's average daily prison population was 7.5 per cent higher than in 1986 (Home Office, 1988b), while in 1987 NACRO's analyses of recent statistical trends in female incarceration rates revealed both that the proportionate use of imprisonment for women had more than doubled in the past ten years, and that women were tending to be sent to prison for less serious offences than men (NACRO, 1987a and b). In March 1988 it was reported that at the end of 1987 'the female [prison and youth custody] population (including those in police cells) was about 65 higher than a year earlier' (Home Office, 1988h:2) and that 'the average sentence length of adult females received from the Crown Court has shown larger proportionate increases than those for adult males' (ibid.:9). Home Office 'Projections of long term trends in the prison population to 1997' asserted in April 1989 that 'the population of females is projected to be around 2,200 in 1997 as compared with 1,800 in 1987 and 1988' (Home Office, 1989a:8). Knowing that increasing numbers of women were going into custody, my informants thought that women–only groups might convince sentencers that there really are some non–custodial options fashioned specially for women.

2 Concern about inappropriate recommendations being made to the courts in the cases of women

This rationale took two major forms:

(a) Too many probation officers and sentencers operate with a welfare model of probation for female offenders which (though it may be justified in terms of women's social circumstances) results in women offenders being made more vulnerable to a custodial sentence if they re-offend in future.

On this rationale the justifications for women's groups were:

(i) That probation officers would be able to recommend a conditional discharge for first-time and other minor offenders and yet *still* offer help with welfare needs by bringing the women's (voluntary) group to clients' attention at the Report stage.

(ii) That availability of a women's group focused on offending behaviour would both remind magistrates that women should not be put on probation unless they have committed an offence liable to a custodial sentence and convince them that, when women *do* merit probation, a well-thought out programme will ensure that attention is focused as much on the offending behaviour as on the social circumstances which might have precipitated it.

(b) When women commit a more serious type of offence the range of realistic and positive non-custodial options for women is very much narrower than that for men, and women's groups (both for voluntary and 11 4(b) attenders) would help redress the imbalance in non-custodial provision between the sexes.

3 The difficulties surrounding Community Service for women

Probation officers claimed that there was a general prejudice against recommending women for Community Service (CS): first, because lack of crèche facilities could raise difficulties (in some cases insuperable, in others imaginary) concerning the woman's ability to complete the order; and second, because it was sometimes considered that the Community Service jobs available were unsuitable for women. (Two contradictory ideologies were at work here. Some probation officers were reluctant to recommend CS because they felt that their women clients would either be given 'women's work' or be sent to agencies where they could take their children and subsequently be unfairly expected to do the CS task *and* mind their children at the same time (cf. Dominelli, 1984). Some male probation officers and supervisors were suspected of refusing to take women unless some traditional 'women's work' was available.) All the officers spoken to were quick to point to the many ironies surrounding CS for women.

> It was argued here recently that when a woman is on Community Service child care should be provided by Social Services, yet no child care is available in this area anyhow. So how could Social Services provide it? Yet it *is* ironic that, if the woman *isn't* given CS because of lack of crèche facilities, she may go to prison and her children go into Care anyhow. They would then cost Social Services much more than the cost of a creche.
>
> (Woman probation officer, Birmingham)
>
> I knew of a woman doing CS who didn't like the job she'd been given – a real traditional woman's job. So she asked if she could go on the Task Force –

decorating, that kind of thing. And the officer in charge arranged it. Then, the first time she went, the Supervisor in charge of the Task Force asked her to take the men's overalls to the launderette. She was furious. It's often not so much the Community Service officers but the supervisors who're prejudiced.

(Senior probation officer, Manchester)

It was to counteract this prejudice and surmount other difficulties that some officers suggested there should be CS officers and CS teams specifically for women.

We need to have a CS officer specifically for women, someone who would go out and get jobs and liaise with Social Services so that the children *could* be looked after.

(ACPO, West Midlands)

4 Women who have been victims of child abuse or domestic violence need a space where they can recover their confidence away from men

A considerable number of women appearing before the courts have been victims of sexual or domestic violence. It was therefore argued that for these women mixed non-custodial programmes, day centres and CS teams are particularly inappropriate, if not downright threatening. Additionally, it was claimed, even where women have not been victims of physical abuse, many have not had the space to develop relationships with adult women outside the home, and they also need to be able to develop their social skills independently of the male dominance that usually prevails in mixed groups.

5 Women on probation are often seen as a 'problem' and therefore women-only groups provide a positive resource for all officers

Male colleagues make sexist jokes about women. 'Oh what goes on in the group? I wouldn't know what to do when they cry!' It's a joke, but it's a *sexist* joke.

(Woman probation officer, Manchester)

So far as women are concerned the fact of being a woman is seen as being a problem. If you take a man and a woman, each with two problems, say alcoholism and mental illness, then being a woman is, in itself, seen as a third problem. . . . Generally speaking, there's a feeling that there's more work with a woman than with a man, that more problems will arise. (The problems are often created by the *men* at home but then it's the woman on probation who comes and presents.) . . . In the Banger Project, when we had a woman we realized that the whole idea had been set up on the assumption that we'd never have a woman. As soon as we had a woman we had to start thinking about separate toilet facilities, different overalls, and *then* we realized that it had all been set up for men.

(Male SPO, Manchester)

Probation officers running women's groups argued that the existence of women-only groups both highlighted the fact that women had different needs to men and provided a general resource for officers who might, for a variety of reasons, feel that they could not make adequate provision for some of those needs.

6 The material and psychological conditions conducive of women's offending are different to those conducive of men's

When talking of their female clients probation officers often made the point that 'their reasons for offending are different. Women are more into survival crimes' (probation officer, Cardiff). These 'different reasons' for offending were primarily defined in terms of material deprivation (poverty and its related poor housing, ill-health and lack of mobility), but there was, additionally, always reference to the related psychological problems rooted both in poverty *and* in the prevailing ideologies of womanhood which still privilege middle-class women as having more of the 'feminine' virtues than working-class women. Concern centred on the increasing numbers of very young girls entering the criminal justice system and the increasing numbers of single parents living in poverty.

> There are so few places for 15 and 16 year old girls to go if they've fallen out with their parents. They're shipped from one unsuitable place to another and we are just not addressing their problems. The intermediate treatment centre is very, very male oriented – martial arts and rock-climbing – and there are no separate facilities for girls. Girls taken into Care for a couple of shoplifting offences may run away and go into prostitution. Or even if they don't abscond, they may just get into prostitution through lack of supervision.
>
> (Male SPO, Manchester; cf. Christina and Carlen, 1985;
> Carlen, 1987 and 1988)

In relation to older women, concern focused on the difficulties they face (as lone mothers with children) in having to deal single-handedly with the variety of agencies supposedly set up to assist them.

> Doctors' receptionists are often *very* difficult to get past. Then there's the DHSS. Women get very frustrated when they phone the DHSS and get passed from person to person. The pips keep going, they run out of 10ps; they get frustrated – smash the phone or the glass in the booth and won't claim. We tell them not to bother phoning, to *go* to the DHSS office. Get there early – so you're first. If you think there's going to be a long wait, take sandwiches and something to drink. We try to get them to avoid being angry, frustrated and then losing out either because they lose their benefits or, worse, get violent with someone.
>
> (Probation officer, Birmingham Women's Group B

The biggest problem for the women who come here is the DHSS. DHSS people often live in middle-class areas and don't realize what poverty is like.

People who don't own phones or can't get to a phone just don't get anywhere. You can go down there and wait for hours. They (and we) just have to
keep on plodding and plodding but the girls are saying, 'I've had enough', and
then they go out and steal. They try and try and then one day they say, 'sod
it', and fiddle the meter or shoplift.

(Woman probation volunteer, Manchester Day Centre A)

Additionally, it was agreed that poverty-stricken women's ability to confront
material deprivation has usually been atrophied both by the hardships of poverty
itself and by a 'women's' upbringing that has not prepared them for the confronta-
tions nowadays integral to welfare state/citizen–client relationships. As one probation officer put it:

The special difficulty for women is that they tend to get stuck in private life.
Even if a man is unemployed and on probation, because he's not expected to
be home with the children (and also because it's OK for a man to be out and
about doing nothing in particular all day) he still seems to get into the public
space more often.

(Probation officer, Cardiff)

Because of this isolation and the lack of confidence accompanying it, some probation officers running women's groups thought that the group filled a major need,
even if the women did nothing more than sit and talk: 'The original idea was to
help the "overspill women" who are very isolated. What they want to do is sit and
talk' (Staffordshire probation officer re Staffs Women's Group B). But more positive activities were also recommended and undertaken.

Assertiveness training can work wonders. One woman changed completely.
Before, she wouldn't go anywhere or do anything. Now she'll get up and go
anywhere.

(Cardiff probation officer re Cardiff Women's Group)

Before I came to the Group I couldn't talk to people. I couldn't mix with
people, but now I can answer back. I'm off probation now, but I shall still
keep coming.

(Kath, ex-probation client and ex-prisoner,
Manchester Women's Group A)

We began with a real core group of offenders, all in real need. Each thought
she was the only person in the world with a suspended sentence. Now they've
become a self-supporting group.

(Staffordshire probation officer re Staffs Women's Group B)

7 Women's groups can supplement the gaps in 'throughcare' provision and provide additional (or sometimes sole!) support for women with drugs, alcohol or mental health problems

The plight of the very young women who pass from residential Care to youth custody and then return to a life of either isolation and deprivation in inner city bedsits or, worse, homelessness and begging on the streets, was described by several youth workers in Birmingham, Manchester and London. A Manchester probation officer explained how these young people are too often rejected by all the relevant agencies.

> If a 15 year old girl is homeless and taken into Care for being in moral danger, she is the responsibility of the Social Services. But if the girl has left school (and the schools often exclude them at the first opportunity) and is sent to Youth Custody, Social Services can go to court, say 'there's nothing else we can do', get the court order discharged, and eventually the problem's passed on to us. Though we may never have had any contact with her.
>
> (Male probation officer, Manchester)

> Young women in Youth Custody Centres are often just abandoned. They need help when they come out.
>
> (Woman SPO, Birmingham)

Women's groups, it was argued, could help these young women, as well as support drug takers, alcoholics and mentally ill women who did not feel they could cope with mixed facilities.

> Women who need help can come to the group even if they're not on probation – it's help without stigma.
>
> (Probation officer, Cardiff Women's Group)

> We're willing to set up special groups as needed – for women on drugs or with alcohol problems.
>
> (Woman probation officer, Staffs Women's Group D)

> We are trying to get women-only groups for drinkers because the reasons why women drink are different. They tend to drink alone – not so much in company, not in pubs. But they are reluctant to come forward because a woman who's a mother is not supposed to drink – there's more disgrace.
>
> (Woman probation officer, Birmingham Women's Group A; cf. Carlen, 1983a)

> I'm not using [heroin] now and that's because of NA [Narcotics Anonymous]. I go there every day. But you need to keep busy. . . . That's why I come here [women's group] too.
>
> (Brenda, ex-prisoner, ex-heroin user, Manchester Women's Group B)

The need for separate facilities for women with drink and drug problems has been stressed again and again, though at the present time such facilities will not be found outside the large conurbations. The Women's Alcohol Centre in North London is thought to be unique.

The Centre was opened in May 1984 and as far as we know is the only resource of its kind in the country. For some time it had been clear to workers at other ARP [Alcohol Recovery Project] facilities that their male-dominated cultures were not allowing women the space or security properly to investigate their problems with alcohol. Often, in fact, the effect was quite counterproductive, allowing women to repeat familiar self-defeating patterns and having negative self-images reinforced. The establishment of a women-only resource came to be seen as essential.

(Alcohol Recovery Project, 1988)

And when I interviewed a worker at the Centre in 1988 she made a point that was to run as a constant refrain through my interviews with co-ordinators of women's groups and women's hostels: 'Lots of women who come here have suffered from incestuous relationships.'

8 Women's groups can help prevent re-offending or offending in future

Five ways in which groups help women keep out of trouble were mentioned by group leaders.

(i)   Focusing on offending behaviour and identifying the situations and types of behaviour which are likely to result in an offence being committed.

(ii) Teaching women how to deal with stressful situations (wind-ups) in ways that will achieve their objectives without landing them in trouble.

(iii) Explaining how the tariff system of sentencing works and the likely consequences of further law-breaking.

(iv) Supporting offenders and ex-prisoners by providing them with friendship and advice.

(v)   Supporting non-offending women at risk of law-breaking because of their adverse social circumstances (e.g. husband/cohabitee in prison, ex-drug users, poverty-stricken lone mothers).

Women in prison often complain that during their sentence nobody ever speaks to them about their crimes. The probation officers who had been running groups focused on offending behaviour stressed that women who commit serious crimes *do* want to discuss them and that, furthermore, those continually in trouble *do* welcome advice about how to change their behaviour patterns.

We exclude first-time offenders and concentrate on the high tariff women. We ask women if they *want* to stop offending. (Some groups forget to do that.) Then we ask them to fill out a questionnaire to identify their problems. In the first group they were all stress-related crimes, family problems, pressures of being single parents, tranquillizer abuse, plus the fact that they were women. Gender *was* raised as an issue.

(Probation officer, Manchester Women's Group A)

When I asked Kath, an ex-member of a Manchester offending-behaviour-focused group, why she still attended (at the drop-in group) she said she needed the advice and support that would help her avoid crime in future.

> I want to get a full-time job and get off the Social, but I've got to sort my money out first and work out if I can manage. Pinching food and clothes for my kids was how I got into trouble. I don't want to go back to that.
>
> (Ex-group member, Manchester Women's Group A)

The women's day centre in Birmingham was also mindful of the fact that recidivist women need help with offending behaviour.

> We try to increase women's understanding of their offending. Role-playing can help. Some women refuse to see their offending as such if it hasn't got a victim. To others we have to explain the tariff system.
>
> (Probation officer, Birmingham Women's Group B)

Ex-drug user Brenda was adamant in her assertion that community support is a necessity for the recovering heroin addict.

> Some people try to do a geographical. That is, they think they can give up drugs by moving. Others think you do a geographical by going to prison – but you can get drugs in prison. The only way you come off the gear is by thinking every day, 'I'm not having any drugs today', and NOT having any. But you do need a crutch or two.
>
> (Brenda, Manchester Women's Group A)

And all the leaders of probation-run women's groups cited two indicators of their success: first, the fact that clients in the groups often ask if they can bring their non-offender friends, and second, that women completing their orders again and again ask to be allowed to continue to attend the group. The reasons? Because even if they resolve to be law-abiding in future, they still daily have to confront the adverse material conditions which were part-cause of the offending behaviour in the first place.

9 Women's groups can promote solidarity amongst previously isolated women and enable them to campaign for better living conditions

Finally, all the women's group leaders knew that talk was not enough. They knew that for lasting effect the groups had to enable the women to generate ways and means of improving their own standard of living and gaining some control over community conditions.

> The group has become financially self-supporting. They run a coffee bar for other people in the building, they make school jumpers for a pound, they do perms at £3.25. To see their egos grow is fantastic. Now someone has put up £1,000 for three of them to go into business together.
>
> (Leader, Staffordshire Women's Group B)

Our long-term aim is to get women to meet each other outside. We want them to be confident enough to manage without us.

(Probation officer, Manchester Women's Group B)

The women develop amazingly. They have taken to organizing themselves in group activities during the children's vacations.

(Probation officer, Birmingham Women's Group A)

We have excellent community relations. We get the council in to talk about repairs. We bring Family Planning in. And I even got all the women to enrol as members of the Child Poverty Action Group [CPAG]. If women go in and say to an official, 'I'm a member of CPAG', they really sit up and take notice.

(Leader, Birmingham Women's Group B)

Activities of probation-run women's groups

As I have already indicated, the women's groups varied in their activities and degree of structure. Here are descriptions of four different types. The Staffordshire group is the least structured, the Manchester one the most, while one of the two Birmingham groups is actually run on the same site as a mixed day centre where the male leader is particularly aware of the problems facing women with children who wish to attend a women's group *and* have the better facilities of a mixed centre.

Staffordshire Women's Group B
(as described by its probation officer leader)

The group runs on Tuesday from 10 to 1, and it *has* saved women from prison. Our magistrates are totally supportive and have given us money, materials and wool. The pre-school children come with Mum and we run a volunteer crèche in the school holidays. The group is open to offenders, wives of male offenders, and at present three members are non-offenders; they had come along to the office as suicidal. The group is open to anyone. The core group is strong enough to cope with any type of offender. We do handicrafts and last Christmas provided a new toy for 28 deprived kids. We also sold toys and provided a superb Christmas party. We do a coffee bar every fortnight – that's a money spinner – and we raise money for group members by doing dressmaking and knitting – we have a knitting machine. Three members are now going into business together. We go on outings – Chester Zoo, Styal Mill, have meals out. They do support each other. They coped with one lady who had hygiene problems and one who was on an indecent abuse charge.

They take an interest in other people's problems. Our one basic rule is that everything is confidential to the group and to their great credit they've kept that rule. They are very aware that the group has kept them out of prison. One girl I had to breach [take back to court for not fulfilling the conditions of the order] and the judge gave her three months to improve before deciding what to do with her. She came to the group and during that three months she turned the corner.

Birmingham Women's Group A, mixed day centre
(as described by the female leader of the women's group and the male SPO in charge of the mixed day centre)

The group runs once a week for 1½ hours. They bring their children, and non-offenders can come as well as prisoners' wives. In fact the funding tends to come under prisoners' wives funding, but they're not mainly prisoners' wives. Activities include pottery sessions, sex education, a careers service for women who want to get back to work; Rape Crisis Centre talks, police talking about rape suites. We have fun trips – like to the Black Country Museum and an outing at Christmas. All but one of the women are white. We had hoped for a greater mixture but we're now trying to run a group for Asian women with men inside. It gets women out of the home and they have taken to organizing themselves quite a bit. For a time we had a male officer and a male Community Service offender running the crèche. It was good to bring in men in a positive light, especially for women who had never experienced men in a caring role.

(Woman leader)

The centre has been running for two years and in the first six months we had few black people and few women. Now black people and women attending are representative for this county. We try to recognize that women may want to do 'women's things', but what usually happens is that at first they gravitate towards catering and traditional women's things but then, with encouragement, turn to woodwork and begin to inquire what the men are doing. A female teacher from the local authority comes in two mornings a week for basic numeracy and literacy. We have a computer. We have also established a link with the local authority Children's Centre so now we can accept women with small children and women can therefore take advantage of this particular court disposal. The Children's Centre will work with a woman if she needs help with parenting and will send a minibus to take the woman and children there. In the main women mixing with men works well. But it helps having the women's group so that women coming to the centre can go there. There is no problem for *us* having women but we recognize that problems are put in their way. For instance, one woman has to get three buses to get here. She gets here at 10.45 (and I am prepared to accept that) and then she has to leave early to get her children from school. Some people would say that she shouldn't be allowed to come, but why not? I think she's showing great commitment and organization to get here under those circumstances. But there must be other women like her who get refused the opportunity because they can't meet the official requirements.

(Male SPO)

Birmingham Women's Group B, run from women's day centre
(as described by the women's group leader)

We take women on Section 11 on Tuesdays and Thursdays (Birmingham West) and Wednesdays and Fridays (Birmingham South). (We try to get them to develop their own social networks; that's why we have divided into West and South). This *is* an alternative to custody. Priority is given to Section 11 women. But most of the women who come here have been used and abused by men. In September we're going to run an 'incest' group. Women who've left can come on Mondays, when there's a drop-in group. Schedule 11 is 30 days – which is 3 months – then they're offered another 3 months. None turn it down. During those two 3 months we provide transport; after that they can still come but they have to provide their own. While they are on Schedule 11 probation pays for their children to go to a nursery. One morning a week is free and easy. They talk amongst themselves. It's lovely for them to have a cup of tea without the children. The other morning is Social Skills – assertiveness – six week course – focusing on offending behaviour – all kinds of people come in to talk – family planning, a vicar, people from the council. We make women aware of everything that's available to them. There are not many groups in this area. Women's groups need nurturing; that's why we provide transport. Some women have been coming for five years. We don't get much re-offending.

Manchester Women's Group
(as described by one of the two women probation officers who
co-ordinated it)

We were only able to run this group once, and then until now [June 1988]
staffing problems have made it impossible for us to run it again. The group
was voluntary but we wanted to sell it to the courts, so we designed a very
structured course and prepared it in our own time in each other's houses in
the evenings. We had a twelve session programme for that group and it ran
from 9 a.m. to 2 p.m. every Thursday. What happened on the group was
confidential. At the end we wrote an assessment with the women and asked
them individually if they then wanted to attend the Drop-In. All but two did.
Women in that group who re-offended tended not to get custody. It was
recognized that groups are good in themselves.

(Co-ordinator)

[Literature on the aims of the group and an impressive documentation of all
meetings (excluding names of participants) were also made available to me. I
quote below from the document (Barrie and Ross, 1987) in which the aims of
the group are set out.]

The aim of the group is to examine in depth women's offending and associated behaviour, both direct and indirect. The topics which are covered . . .
include the following:

1 Identification of, and coping mechanisms for dealing with, stress.
2 Examination of individual women's self-control in an attempt to reduce
  further offending.
3 Depression and tranquilliser abuse.
4 Assertiveness Training.
5 Problem solving.
6 Issues relating to appropriate parenting skills

Barriers to the development of probation-run women's groups

Although all the women probation officers I spoke to had great enthusiasm for
developing specialized work with women offenders, they all thought at the time of
interview (1988) that it was unlikely that the work would be much extended in the
near future. The women's groups, for instance, appeared to be under threat from
four major sources: familial ideologies that still propagate the notion that a
woman's place is in the home; male chauvinism within probation together with a
prejudice against group work in general; current government policies on criminal

justice that are inclined more towards punishment than towards the rehabilitation of offenders and the prevention of crime; and contemporary conservative ideologies that favour individualistic rather than collectivist responses to social problems and, accordingly, finance entrepreneurial private profit-making enterprises rather than co-operative schemes to improve public amenities.

1 A woman's place is in the home

The possessiveness and exclusionary practices that some men still engage in with regard to their wives' social and public lives have already been documented (e.g. Hunt, 1980; Carlen, 1983a and 1988). In 1986, for instance, I was told by a woman on probation in Staffordshire that she could not join the probation-run women's groups she had been advised to attend because 'He [her husband] will not let me go out on my own or with other women.' By 1988 many women on probation still appeared to be in the same situation.

> Some women can't come because their husbands are not prepared to look after the children.
>
> (Probation officer, Cardiff)

> A couple of husbands have said that they're not willing to let their children go on the group's outing at Christmas.
>
> (Probation officer, Women's Group A, Manchester)

2 Prejudices against women's groups within probation

> Men seem to have a voyeuristic interest in what goes on in a women's group. One magistrate asked me, 'What happens in a women's group? I want to see a video of what goes on before I suggest to a woman that she goes to one.' A Chief Probation Officer (not in this service, but not so far from here) said, 'Women's group? What's that? Some sort of group for gay probation officers?'
>
> (Woman probation officer)

Two major 'service-based' barriers to the development of women's groups were identified: a strong streak of male chauvinism and a residual resistance to group work *per se*.

Several officers made the point that it was unrealistic to expect the probation service to recognize the special needs of women clients when women officers themselves still receive a raw deal in the service.

> Over half the officers here are women but there is only one woman senior out of a group of fifteen. The women don't go for promotion and the managers don't easily recognize career breaks. The pattern of probation working doesn't make it easy to do job shares.
>
> (Woman SPO, Manchester)

Since 1978 I've been talking about assertiveness groups for women probation officers but it's only now being taken seriously. There's no formal structure for talking about careers but *informally* men are encouraged to apply for posts as Seniors. Women SPO's can facilitate – they *can* keep women's groups on the agenda.

(Woman SPO, Birmingham)

This lack of awareness of 'women's issues' was, according to a West Midlands woman manager, often apparent in other areas of probation:

We [women] need to hold to the issue of women's invisibleness because if we don't no one else will. Whatever the men say, many of them hold stereotypes about women's roles and problems. For instance, in a male hostel run by a female SPO recently she was very concerned to find that the residents of that hostel had fathered four children in a year – and were taking no responsibility for them. So she raised with them questions of contraception. But this wasn't done by the male officers involved in the other hostels because (apparently) they think contraception is a women's issue – women are responsible for pregnancy.

But, whatever the suspicions of women probation officers concerning the underlying sexism of their male colleagues, all leaders of women's groups stressed that their clients usually came from referrals by the same probation officers (both male and female) and that *some* officers never made referrals to the group.

Some officers think that a women's group is a bit racy. Some officers are against groups *per se*.

(Woman probation officer, Cardiff)

We're not totally group–oriented as a service. There's no space for group work on form 30.

(Woman SPO, Manchester)

So why don't women probation officers do something about the less than equitable treatment of women in probation? The answer is simple. At times when *all* welfare oriented services are under threat, 'People are often afraid to raise questions of equity because then the original scheme might be stopped altogether' (Woman SPO, Birmingham).

3 Government policy of punitive rather than supportive non-custodial penalties

When in July 1988 the Government published its discussion document, *Punishment, Custody and the Community* (Home Office, 1988c), it clearly indicated that the stated aim of reducing the prison population was not to be achieved by an increase in supportive and remedial services for offenders. On the contrary. The argument was that the prison population would only be reduced if sentencers were to have more confidence in the non-custodial alternatives. To induce judges to impose more non-custodials, therefore, all existing non-custodial programmes should be stiffened and rigidly enforced. A range of other, new non-custodials was proferred for discussion: e.g. electronic monitoring, curfew or house arrest, and tracking an offender's whereabouts. Throughout the document there was an implication that probation in particular had been at fault in relation to the implementation of non-custodial programmes:

> The Home Office will be asking the probation service to review its activities and to develop a programme of action in each area aimed at ensuring that the supervision of serious offenders in the community commands the confidence of the public and the courts.
>
> (Home Office, 1988c:5)

And, as Tony Ward wrote in November 1988, mention in the paper of private sector involvement in non-custodial penalties was clearly a warning to any probation officers inclined to resist the move from *rehabilitation* in the community to punishment therein (Ward, 1988). Professor Terence Morris, writing in the same edition of the Howard League's *Criminal Justice*, agreed

> The warning words . . . are contained in . . . paragraph 4.4 of Part IV of the Green Paper which refers to a new organisation to 'organise punishment in the community'. . . . It goes on to suggest, 'The new organisation could contract for services from the Probation Service . . .'.
>
> (Morris, 1988)

Yet, according to my 1988 informants, the anti-rehabilitationist tone of the Green Paper only made explicit what had been known to probation officers for a long time: that their rehabilitative and deterrent work had been downgraded by a government bent on bringing the pains of imprisonment into the community or, as Barbara Hudson has put it, turning 'alternatives to custody' into 'alternative custody' (Hudson, 1987). Such a policy has obviously had effects on the degree of priority given to women's groups. Officers from both Manchester and the West Midlands complained that although their services had a *policy* on women's issues, there was no service-wide structure for its implementation.

> There are many *policies*, but the mechanisms to put them into practice just don't exist. Whenever there are cuts, specialist services suffer because there is no overall view of service delivery to clients.
>
> (Male SPO, West Midlands)

> We are trying to get a co-ordinated policy and in this office we've always had money for women's groups. But there's no central policy – or rather there *is* a policy but no structure to put it into practice.
>
> (Woman SPO, Manchester)

Explanations for this lack of structure varied, though the two main ones related to, first, the reluctance of the service to impose rigid methods of working on professionals who have traditionally been allowed a degree of latitude in their diagnosis and 'treatment' of their clients' needs; and, second, the lack of funds to implement policies which, because of governmental transcarceral ideologies, are given no priority if they are supportive, remedial and regulative rather than primarily punitive. The effects of these two factors on women's groups were to be seen both in problems of staffing and in the lack of provision of creches and transport for the women clients whom they might have benefited.

> Our running the group was in line with the regional plan yet we got no space [time] in which to run the group. We had no video-material provided centrally. We've only done the group once. We should have a women's group running all the time, as the numbers of high tariff women have risen, but my caseload was 45 and we just couldn't run it again.
>
>   (Woman probation officer, Manchester Women's Group A)

> The difficult bit is keeping the impetus going. We've got the expertise but now we've a staffing problem. But we do intend to run it again. We have an activities budget so we have money to do things, but we would also need money for staffing a creche.
>
>   (Woman SPO, Manchester Women's Group A)

> The group was set up two years ago when we had two officers interested in group work. But no one is *asked* to run a group. It depends on the officer's own interest. Management is now considering we're spending too much time with it. It needs two people but management feels there should only be one officer. The group is only recommended by some officers, others never make referrals at all. We are not given a budget and I think that indicates that the group is *not* high priority in the service. We have to get *ad hoc* budgeting and yet we are supposed to be teaching the women about budgeting. We need to be able to demonstrate that the women can organize themselves independently yet we can never tell them how much the group has to spend.
>
>   (Woman probation officer, Birmingham Women's Group A)

Officers were well aware that the degree of voluntarism allowed to probation officers in their adoption of group work (or other new ways of working) raised problems of equity in relation to their service delivery:

> The lack of structure in probation means that things get done very much on an *ad hoc* basis which also means that we can seem very inconsistent to clients.
>
>   (Woman SPO, Manchester)

At the same time, it was claimed that 'people are often afraid to raise questions of equity because then the original scheme might be stopped' (Woman SPO, West Midlands Women's Group C). The downgrading of the groups, it was feared, also resulted in a lack of professional recognition for the (usually women) officers who ran them, and although it is unlikely that the officers who have run women's groups have done so for personal advancement, the West Midlands woman ACPO to whom I spoke was quite properly concerned about the issue of rewarding innovative ways of working.

> Management in probation does have to address the issue of how to show recognition of people's work in new areas. Shop floor workers need to know that their work is being recognized.
>
> (Woman ACPO, West Midlands)

Magistrates could also be lukewarm about women's groups:

> I write to all new magistrates offering to talk with them about women's issues but there's a very poor take-up. The charitable view is that they're very busy; the uncharitable view is that they're not really interested.
>
> (Woman SPO, Manchester)

A male SPO touched on similar issues of recognition when he summed up the position of women's groups in Manchester.

> As far as women's groups are concerned, I think they've been downgraded. At one office there was a very successful women's group and the officer was, well, not exactly forced to disband it, but told it was low priority, told it was to be done in her own time. It was *not* seen as an alternative to custody; preventative work was discredited. But the CPO here now is very keen on preventative work, so it may be coming back.
>
> (Male SPO, Manchester)

4 'There is no such thing as society, only individuals and families' (Prime Minister Thatcher, 1988)

The move away from preventative work in probation was also linked with the ethic of individualism propagated by central government – an ethic which refuses to acknowledge that certain crimes might indeed be individualistic responses to *social* problems.

> Another problem is that this centre serves two areas – one Labour and one Conservative. If someone needs a social resource and lives in D— then, tough! It's a Tory Council.
>
> (Male SPO, West Midlands)

> We work in the local community but it's not recognized. Probation nowa-days is about the nuts and bolts of court work. The number of reports we do can be counted but the deterrent value of community work can't be measured. If we do community work there's no follow through and we're therefore not supported in the deterrent work we do.
>
> (Woman SPO, Manchester)

Repeatedly it was stressed that the probation service had to give priority to court work and that other work could only be done, as one officer put it, 'as a sideline'. Yet many of my informants held to a principled belief that only an increase in preventative and rehabilitative work *now* would lead to lower levels of crime in the future. These were the officers who were prepared to give up their own time to run women's groups. But they had to do good by stealth. For one of their major problems was that, because of the run-down in community provision in general, probation-run groups could gradually come to be seen as a welcome resource for the whole community. Not only did women clients who had successfully completed their orders still want to attend, they wanted to bring their friends and neighbours too! Where officers were operating such community-oriented provision, they were convinced that to the extent that this was preventative work it could be defined as being a proper (though marginal) concern of probation. Be that as it may, the continued existence of their groups was constantly under threat. In sum, they had to confront the irony that while women constitute only a small proportion of all known offenders, and prevailing ideologies result in community punishment for offenders rather than community provision for *all*, probation's effective preventative work with women (and others) will continue to be downgraded.

> Again and again numbers is a problem. We don't want more women in the criminal justice system, but until there *are* it's unlikely there'll be much done for them. Women's issues are not a major policy issue at the moment simply because there are not enough women in the criminal justice system. If women's groups become successful they tend to discontinue them, because being successful means that women want to continue attending after their order is finished; they want to bring their friends and then probation is filling in the gaps in social provision in general. So *then* it's seen as not being really probation work and is discontinued. It's ironical really.
>
> (Male SPO, Manchester)

Probation officers are in a double bind. Well appraised of a sentencing tendency to push women up tariff by putting them on probation in recognition of their welfare needs, they do NOT wish to continue to draw low tariff women into the probation net. On the other hand, they recognize that in some extremely deprived inner city areas probation may be the only service offering the type of provision that might prevent destitute young girls and overburdened older women from committing crime in the future. In these circumstances it is fortunate (and admirable) that, despite their awareness of the paradoxes, officers continue to struggle to put women's issues more squarely on the rehabilitative agenda. Even so, the women's group leaders I talked with were all aware of the limits to group work. Committed though they were to the extension of women-only groups, they stressed that probation officers should not feel obliged to fill in the gaps in community provision for non-offenders, that their proper job is with offenders, and that even for their statutory clients women's groups cannot remedy women offenders' major problems of poverty, poor education, unemployment and inadequate housing. Yet, though many female offenders themselves do not wish to live on the poverty line of DSS benefits they often cannot do otherwise either because of their lack of education or because of the dearth of employment opportunities coupled with the reluctance of employers to take on ex-offenders.

Education

The major provider of education specifically for ex-prisoners is NACRO, which during 1986–7 had 3,766 students attending its 14 voluntary education projects. Forty four per cent of participants were female, and although 'there are no women-only projects' (reply to telephoned query to NACRO Information, November 1988), 'creches are provided at several centres to help young mothers attend' (NACRO, 1987c).

From NACRO Annual Report 1986–7

Most students are unemployed, often for a long time. The centres provide a constructive use of time and boost self-confidence as well as skills. Offenders and non-offenders mix together and are treated alike, as students. . . . The staff aim to create a place which is a real educational community to which all contribute. . . . The largest group of students is aged under 25, but a substantial minority is considerably older. Around a third are women who have the opportunity to try non-traditional skills. . . . The centres also provide advice on access to mainstream education courses for offenders generally, and particularly those leaving prison. The National Education Advisory Service deals with a further 500 enquiries a year, predominantly from prisoners preparing for release. Over half of those wanting financial help got it, including around 50 NACRO grants. Only 15% failed or withdrew from courses on which they were helped to get places.

(NACRO, 1987c:8–9)

NACRO's Women Prisoners Resource Centre (WPRC) was set up in 1984 as a referral centre 'for London women who are or who have recently been in custody' (WPRC, 1986) and in 1985–6 had 18 inquiries from women prisoners and ex-prisoners concerned with improving their education.

From Women Prisoners Resource Centre Annual Report 1985–6

WPRC collects and provides written information for . . . women so they have a better idea of what is available. Women are referred on to local adult education advice centres where they can get individual attention on finding and getting on to the right course, e.g. North London Education Project, Camden Adult Learning Centre, LEO (Lambeth Education), Westminster Education Advice Centre. The centres can give the women more specific information on grant applications and child care facilities.

(WPRC, 1986:16)

One of the projects mentioned most frequently by staff of the women's prisons and by women ex-prisoners themselves as providing an attractive combination of education, support and accommodation was the North London Education Project.

Extract from North London Education Project Report 1984–6

We are able to offer accommodation to 30 residents at any one time. . . . The accommodation is high quality, each resident being allocated a study bedroom and sharing a kitchen and bathroom. . . . [Separate accommodation *is* available for women.] Every student is allocated a Personal Tutor who provides educational support and practical guidance. . . . Residents may stay for as long as they are studying, and through a number of nominations from local agencies . . . many are permanently rehoused on leaving. Our Education Day Centre in North Hackney is open to all members of the community, whether or not they are offenders. . . . One of the Project's Education Officers is based at North London Further Education College and provides a link into mainstream education, as well as providing counselling and support for the Project's residential students.

Some residential students

Carmen
Carmen joined the Project in August 1985. At 18 years old she was one of the youngest members of the Project. Carmen had experienced a very difficult adolescence – her mother died when she was 12 and she was taken into local authority care. During the next few years she became progressively involved with the hard drug scene and was a heroin addict. At the age of 17 Carmen

---

entered the Ley Community (a thereapeutic Drug Rehabilitation Centre) where she successfully completed their 9-month programme. On leaving this community Carmen enrolled at a local F.E. college for a course of 'O' levels. This, however, broke down. She was attracted by the level of educational support of the Project and by the prospect of pursuing the Sports Management Course at North London College. This proved to be a successful choice and Carmen's year at the Project has been used constructively and energetically. Her course was passed with several credits and distinctions. She completed a British Amateur Weight Lifting Association leader's certificate, she was offered several full-time jobs and has now taken the first step in her career in Sports Management. She has been nominated by the Project to a permanent flat to which she will shortly move. Carmen's vitality has enabled her to be involved in a wide range of activities and projects. For instance, she organised a women's football day in Hackney which attracted a great deal of media interest. From this event Carmen has gone on to organise and manage a women's football team in Hackney.

Ngozi

Ngozi was a young woman who, through a severe lack of confidence and social skills, only found acceptance within a group who were involved in prostitution and other criminal activities. She eventually received a custodial sentence. Whilst in Cookham Wood in 1983 she became fired with an enthusiasm for studying and education that has never left her.

Starting at quite a low level of literacy Ngozi, with the help of the Prison Education Department, took and passed Pitmans Elementary English Language followed later in the year by RSA English Language Stage 1. She became determined to pursue her studies when she was released and consequently applied and was accepted at the Project in January 1984.

She continued to improve on her English and Maths for the rest of that academic year and then embarked on a course of 'O' levels which she took in June 1985. Her hard work and talents were rewarded with 'O' level passes in English Language, Sociology and Psychology.

During the summer of 1985 Ngozi went to live and work on a kibbutz in Israel for 4 months. On her return she entered for 'A' level English Literature and 'A' level Law. Yet again she was successful, passing both subjects in the summer of 1986.

After 2½ very successful years with the Project, Ngozi was rehoused through one of our nominations with Circle 33 Housing Trust. Her educational career is still continuing as she has entered for 'A' level Philosophy and RSA Typing. Ngozi is also working for the Citizens Advice Bureau on a voluntary basis.

(North London Education Project, 1986)

North London Education Project has been chosen for extended mention here not only because it is an example of the best type of education provision for ex-offenders, provision, that is, catering also for the fundamental needs of comfortable and worry-free housing and support in the often lonely business of adult education. It also faces the continuous problems of funding that confront other ex-offender projects, and this lack of resources particularly affects their work with certain types of offender, especially women. They cannot, for instance, take drug takers straight from prison simply because they are insufficiently staffed to give ex-drug takers the intensive support they need.

> We exclude no one because of their crime. We have to look particularly closely at violent offenders but we take them, and we have taken arsonists. We can't take drug takers straight from prison. We have what we call a six months rule – they have to live in the community for six months. This rule is based on our experience that people coming off drugs (or drink) have enough to cope with just coming off and staying off without having to start with education, and education is what we're about. But after six months we'll take referrals from a drug rehabilitation centre.
>
> (Woman worker, NLEP)

This is fair enough from the standpoint of NLEP. With few staff they have to concentrate on their primary objective of educational provision. However, in view of the fact that there are so few drug rehabilitation centres, it does mean that many drug takers will never reach the stage when they can take advantage of the provision that NLEP and other projects offer. Furthermore, although two of the few rules of the Project prohibit racist and sexist behaviour, and the Project explicitly promotes an equal opportunities policy, people with certain physical disabilities cannot attend the Nevill Road site. Lack of crèche facilities (on site and locally) together with a lack of accommodation for mothers and children mean that for many female ex-prisoners participation in the Project is just not feasible.

> We haven't got 'disabled' access so we couldn't have disabled people. We do have separate provision for women and at their interviews we always ask if they want to be in mixed or single accommodation. We also keep spaces for women – we don't fill up any vacant women's spaces with men. [See Chapter 3 for commentary on the hostels that *do* fill up vacant women's places with men.] But so many of the women are single mothers and we have no provision for mothers and children. One of the project leaders went to talk to the women at Cookham Wood [prison] recently and they gave her a really hard time because there was no provision for children here. It's a 'no' area for women with children, provision for ex-prisoners is.
>
> (Woman worker, NLEP)

Ever since the inception of the Day Centre we have wanted to provide Crèche facilities for single parents. Both of the Day Centre's funders (ILEA and London Boroughs Grant Unit) are unable to provide funds for this purpose but we are very fortunate in having been offered the services of Hackney Mobile Creche Unit. This Crèche Unit provides us with crèche facilities for 12 hours per week . . . but . . . are only in a position to provide such a service for a limited period of time while we seek permanent funding. As yet there is no clear indication as to from where such funding might come. We see this as a very high priority, and will do all in our power to secure this money.

(North London Education Project, 1986)

But at the time I visited the Project in summer 1988, it was already under further theat from three different directions – the Social Fund clauses of the 1986 Social Security Act which had become operative in April 1988; the impending abolition of the Inner London Education Authority (ILEA) which had funded the basement Education Day Centre; and the new housing legislation (Housing Act 1988).

Present government policies are undermining the Project on all sides. The working of the Social Fund is going to come down heavy on people wanting to move on. It will make it difficult for them to get money to furnish their own accommodation. ILEA going will cut off the money for the basement and the new Housing Act will most likely result in our losing our nominations for Housing Association accommodation.

(Male project worker)

Work

The rise, since 1979, in the number of people who are out of work has hit the employment prospects of people with an offending background particularly hard. It is estimated that the number of people known to probation officers who are jobless is in excess of 70%, rising in areas of higher unemployment to nearly 90%. In some areas, over half the people on probation officers' case loads have been out of work for more than a year and qualify as long-term unemployed. . . . We therefore consider that having a job is the single most important factor in the resettlement of offenders and prevention of crime; that success in getting and keeping a job will determine, more than anything else, whether or not the individual will stay clear of future trouble with the law.

(NACRO, 1987d:5)

The major agencies concerned with obtaining employment for people with criminal records are NACRO and Apex together with a number of local and smaller charities such as New Bridge in the Greater London Area. NACRO provides Youth Training Schemes for young people who have been in trouble with the law, as well as Community Programmes which in 1988 had filled around 16,000 places, half with people known to have been in prison (NACRO, 1988b). In 1987–8 23 per cent of the participants in NACRO Community Programmes and 10 per cent of those contacting New Bridge were female.

Overall, I found it difficult to get information concerning a special awareness of women's employment needs, the most usual comment from people working in the criminal justice and penal systems being that 'work isn't the *major* problem for women. They have too many others – children, housing and personal relationships' (Prison Department official). The Women Prisoners' Resource Centre's Biennial Report 1987–9 highlighted some of the particular prejudices faced by women and, like other organizations, indicated an awareness that women searching for employment are best served by agencies with a special orientation towards dealing with women's employment problems.

> WPRC collects information on a range of different centres and schemes offering training and employment skills for offenders. We try to make sure that women are not confined to traditionally female areas by building links with organisations like Women and Trades or Camden Training Centre both of whom offer advice and training to women in non-traditional skills such as electronics, plastering, welding and motor mechanics. . . . Women are often not considered to be breadwinners in their own right, and we would like to see the balance redressed here, with employment advice and training for women given equal status. We are keen for prison pre-release courses to be prioritised and include sections in these areas.
>
> (WPRC, 1989a)

Three organizations which are especially geared to women offenders' work requirements are Women's Motor Mechanics Workshop Ltd, Clean Break and CAST.

Women's Motor Mechanics Workshop Ltd

The Women's Motor Mechanics Workshop Ltd is a women-run project in South London, set up by women as a training workshop offering courses in car mechanics. The courses are open to all women who live in Greater London though priority is given to applicants with no previous training who also fall into one or more of the following categories: ex-prisoners, women with criminal records, black and ethnic minority women, and single parents. Over forty women each year pass through the project, which provides each trainee with a weekly allowance to cover the cost of fares, tool kit, meals and laundry. Child-minding, day nursery, after-school and school-holiday care costs can also be paid to trainees with children up to the age of 11. A three month work placement is run for everyone. None the less, when in late 1988 I talked with three of the project's staff, they could still enumerate a vast number of difficulties confronting both the project and the women who successfully complete its courses.

Women don't have to be referred, they can refer themselves. We give priority to women who would otherwise have a hard time getting a job, for example, black women, single parents, ex-prisoners. We don't have a crèche but we can give them money for child care. Women like this scheme because (1) there's no prejudice; (2) the hours are right if they've got children; (3) they get help with numeracy if that's a problem; and (4) they get help with building up confidence.

The people who fund us *are* interested in the numbers game; that is, in the number of people leaving here who get employment. Recently we've appointed an employment officer to go round and search for jobs. There's still a lot of prejudice. Men just don't think women can be mechanics. One woman went for a job when she'd finished the scheme and they offered her a job filing and answering the phone. We *do* find people who are liberal enough to take women with a record but basically if you're a woman you have to be twice as good. The market has been distorted by all the cheap labour, YTS and other schemes. They'll take a woman on a training scheme but then don't want her when she's finished it.

At the end of the course they are semi-skilled mechanics. Many then go on to further training in colleges. They take City and Guilds Parts 1, 2 and 3.

We can't really take disabled people. For instance, we have no one here with sign language. We can't take arsonists or people on probation. We can take people straight from prison but we're really most accessible to women in the London area. Then there's the big problem of homelessness. We can help women with child-minding but not with problems about getting their children out of Care.

Since April [1988] women on social security have been even poorer. We used to give them £10 plus, but now we can't give them more than £5 in cash each week. Though we can give luncheon vouchers. It does mean that in order to complete the course women have to endure a lot of poverty.

(Interview with three staff members of Women's Motor
Mechanics Workshops 1985)

Clean Break Theatre Company

Clean Break Theatre Company was set up by prisoners in Askham Grange in 1979. Jenny Hicks, one of the founder members, tells how it came about:

We decided to do plays written for women by women and, fortunately, we were lucky enough to have the support and encouragement of the woman

Governor and a feminist teacher. The majority of officers, however, were very much against us working in this way. Clean Break was seen as being anarchic; women actually having fun, making decisions for themselves and doing something positive with their prison experience. The prison experience is so extreme, degrading and humiliating that prisoners' initial sense of guilt and shame is soon replaced by feelings of injustice and alienation from the society which can treat them so. It is for this reason that ex-prisoners need to help each other. Clean Break is successful because we are self-organised. . . . However, through lack of adequate funds, prisoner-run groups like Clean Break and CAST are always working on a shoe string – as when, for instance, Clean Break played one time in Liverpool and the whole cast lived off the proverbial bag of chips!

(Hicks and Carlen, 1985:134, 136)

Yet, despite the struggles for acceptance and finance, Clean Break has survived and, as these two extracts from their 1986–7 Report indicate, has survived triumphantly. Regular writing and improvisation workshops, together with public performances all over the UK and in the United States, have provided innumerable ex-prisoners with the opportunities to develop their talents in a supportive company.

Another exciting period of growth for CLEAN BREAK. After the appointment of our new administrator, Celia Willoughby, we had Gilli Mebarek's national tour of TREADING ON MY TALE; the tour of the USA and London for THE SIN EATERS; the forming of the new Creative Writing Workshop led by Ann Mitchell and Kate Hall and the crowning event in February of the hugely successful performance of women prisoner and ex-prisoner poetry and prose at the RSC Barbican Theatre which filled the auditorium with delighted audience and the stage with actresses from the Clean Break, National Theatre and Royal Shakespeare companies. Thirty five performers in total and a full house out front.

For me personally the most exciting part of our recent work was the writing of THE SIN EATERS: working with Jennifer Hicks, Sarah Newton and director Ann Mitchell on the development of this piece set in Durham H-wing and reaching some parts of the past one really didn't want to reach. The end result was its own reward. Ann had asked us to concentrate on the 'essence' of the experience felt in H-wing and this brought a delicate and sometimes very painful honesty to the whole process but in the end what we had was a very valid, valuable and rich piece of work. After our opening try-out before 70 friends gathered in the Kennedy room of the Irish Centre in Camden, Jennifer Hicks and I flew off for a wonderful five weeks of contact making, networking and experience-sharing on our tour of the States. Greeted with open hearted friendship wherever we went, we performed in Boston and New York, spent a week in the Mitchellville Correctional Facility, Iowa, where we held theatre workshops with the women prisoners, performed SIN EATERS to loud and constant approval and then simply talked and talked and talked about the whole subject of crime and punishment. Finally we toured to California where we met women working in the same field of endeavour: most impressively Remember Our Sisters Inside (or ROSI), whose tireless founder, Sharon, after ten years in a Californian jail runs a network of women prisoner artists from her sick bed on only a few dollars welfare. We met so many powerful and active women that we were fired with a vigour and excitement that I'm sure lives on. Back in London, our tour of local venues brought good reviews but small audiences, leading us to think that perhaps London had had enough of us! The crowds at the Barbican however proved that such was not the case. The Creative Writing Workshop is clearly the way forward, bringing new people, ideas and interest to the company – with so much good work to come.

(Jacki Holborough, 1987)

1986 was for me the best year I ever had with Clean Break. Celia and Jenny were behind me all the way, during the writing, rehearsing and performing of my play *Treading on My Tale*. It was such an opportunity for me – there were people who believed in me enough to let me try a one-woman show, a very hard thing to achieve. But despite the traumas we did it, and achieved an excellent, powerful, truthful account of one woman's fight against the system. For me, being able to perform the play to the patients of Mosside Special Hospital was an unforgettable experience. It was their story too – each person there had been through the same or similar situations and our talk with them afterwards was very rewarding; three people have kept in contact since. I also received a letter from a woman who had been my Probation Officer some years ago, saying she had heard about the play and how amazed she was that I hadn't overdosed and died by now. She was so surprised I was actually not only alive and well but doing something worthwhile.

Thanks to Clean Break, without them I'd have been either inside or due back in. Instead I haven't been arrested for 18 months. An enormous achievement for Clean Break's past residential recidivist.

(Gilli Mebarek, 1987)

CAST

In 1981 an ex-prisoner from Holloway set up another ex-prisoner-organised project. With the help of the education department at Holloway she formed

The Creative and Supportive Trust (known as CAST) a centre to give space, facilities and support to women who want to develop creative talents which will, eventually, enable them to become financially self-supporting – though always the emphasis is upon women's need for intrinsic satisfaction rather than the pursuit of profit.

(Hicks and Carlen, 1985:136)

Occupying two storeys in a house in North-west London, CAST offers information, support and workshops to women who have been in prison, drug or alcohol rehabs or psychiatric units. Workshops in knitted textiles, screen printing, photography, pottery and art give opportunities both to learn new skills and make some money. Most importantly, CAST offers a drop-in service to women who need time, space and sympathetic counselling to work through their post-prison problems. CAST's major strength is that it is run by women ex-prisoners who know just how long it can take to regain self-confidence after release from prison, who know that ex-drug users can need support long after they have kicked their habits, and who know, too, that without some place where newly released ex-prisoners can learn to confront successfully an often uncaring officialdom, some may soon come to believe that it does not matter whether or not they stay out of trouble (and gaol) in the future. The especial quality of CAST's work is well brought out in the following testimony which compared CAST's supportive approach to Community Service in an all-woman environment with the more punitive regime of a mixed CS team where sexism had flourished unchecked.

When my appeal came through my six months sentence was quashed, and I received 240 hours Community Service, I thought I'd never finish it. A lot of ex-prisoners feel you are better off doing your time than having all the hassle of Community Service, I wondered if they were right.

My first assignment was painting and decorating. I thought, 'good I can learn something from this', I did. You're not allowed to be late, be ill, or have personal or home problems. You are there to work, it's punishment, it must come before anything else in your life. If you want time off for an interview, 'tough', you can't go, unless you want to go back to court.

Working with practically all guys was also a problem. Some had the attitude that a girl with a record had to be easy 'Let's see which one can get her first'. Some did not take refusal very lightly.

Now if you had a male supervisor you knew most of your time would go into making cups of tea and washing up. Men's jobs were out of the question, such as climbing a ladder and painting windows, he'd prefer to make a guy afraid of heights go up there rather than a girl who doesn't mind. I then progressed to gardening – well, weeding and making yet more cups of tea.

I asked my Probation Officer if I could work for a women's group and suggested CAST (Creative and Supportive Trust), for female ex-prisoners. It was arranged and off I went. The first thing I noticed when walking in the door was having a friendly face smile and say 'good morning' rather than 'You're five minutes late!'.

The work I did included office duties, attending classes, supporting and helping women with problems. It was nice to fit in, make friends and work as a team and to actually feel you want to do it rather than you have to. It's also good to know you can go there when you have a problem. My hours were flexible, if I could only manage a couple of hours one day I would make up for it the next.

Being a group for ex-prisoners they understood the fact that doing Community Service does not keep you out of trouble, but having the time to get on with your life and being able to deal with problems arising, having time to look for work and generally fitting into society certainly does help. It was great being able to go to a place and be an equal rather than being treated like a naughty child in detention. That way I enjoyed my time there, made friends, worked to the best of my ability, learned some interesting things and worked up a bit of self-confidence to try and work elsewhere. If I had not worked for a group like CAST I'm sure I would have ended back in prison and that wouldn't have been any good to anyone especially me.

(Jeanine Cresswell, 1987)

Researching the all-women groups and projects was the most enjoyable and heartening of the investigative work undertaken for this book. Meeting women living, learning and working together to overcome oppression, discrimination and the effects of some of their own earlier mistakes and misfortunes opened up a vision of so much more that could be done to enable women (and men) in trouble to remake their lives. Chapter 5, therefore, will first provide a summary discussion of the alternatives to women's imprisonment and then outline a strategy for the abolition of women's imprisonment in its present form.

5
Women's imprisonment: towards abolition

I thought how unpleasant it is to be locked out; and I thought how it is worse perhaps to be locked in.

(Virginia Woolf, *A Room of One's Own*,
first published 1929, in Woolf, 1963:37)

Virginia Woolf's reflection on being denied access (as a woman) to the library of an Oxford College in 1928 is an apposite one with which to introduce these concluding thoughts about alternatives to women's imprisonment in the last decade of the twentieth century. For a majority of women locked up in our prisons today are women who have been denied access to decent housing, worthwhile jobs and realistic educational opportunity. Once they have been in prison their options on housing, jobs and education are narrowed still further. Yet the investigations reported in Chapters 3 and 4 convince me, first, that the major way forward for women in trouble is through all-women housing and other types of supportive associations; and, second, that reductionist policies on women's imprisonment are in themselves insufficient for reducing the female prison population. This concluding chapter will therefore be divided into three. The first part will draw on research done in California in 1987 in order to describe some American prison and post-prison projects and services which, if introduced into the UK, might go towards undoing some of the harm that prison does. The second will argue for special and separate projects for women – from sentencing perspectives based on a women's jurisprudence (see Heidensohn, 1986; Stang-Dahl, 1988; Wheeler *et al.*, 1989) to women's accommodation schemes and supportive groups. The underlying argument will be twofold: first, that in rebuilding their lives women in trouble should resist official attempts to squeeze them into existing (male-dominated) structures of logic and dominance; second, that we should struggle to forge women-wise institutions steeped in the knowledge that when women stand before the law we stand as female citizens with needs and experiences which are often very different to those of our male counterparts. Finally, the chapter will close with an abbreviated version of a lecture delivered to the Prison Reform Trust on a strategy for the abolition of women's imprisonment.

Reforming women's prisons

As I shall be stating again later on in this chapter, I am not a prison 'abolitionist' in the sense that I can easily envisage a time when it will not be deemed necessary to lock up certain offenders as a matter of public safety. And, even if I could foresee such a time, the present disgraceful state of British prisons would still provoke me into thinking that in the meantime it is in everyone's interest to bring into our gaols those minimum standards of legality, living conditions and humanitarianism which might limit the damage that prison does. However, in recent years innumerable campaigning groups and authors have listed what needs to be done to reform prisons in general (see Stern, 1989 for the most recent and authoritative account) and the women's prisons in particular (see the Women in Prison Manifesto in Carlen *et al.*, 1985:187–9; Casale, 1989:100–16). Here, therefore, I shall merely discuss three very attainable reforms – reforms which would transform women's experience of penal custody. They are: (1) the setting up of a legal framework for prisons and a specialist legal service for women prisoners; (2) the establishment of a network of halfway houses for imprisoned drug addicts and their babies; and (3) the setting up of visitors' centres at every prison. All of these reforms would be costly, though not so *very* costly if the abolitionist strategy which I propose at the end of this chapter were to be followed – and the women's prison population to fall from 1,800 to around 100!

1 A legal framework for prisons and a specialist legal service for women prisoners

Since 1985, San Francisco attorney Ellen Barry, representing the Legal Services for Prisoners Organization, has filed a series of successful class action suits aimed at improving care for pregnant women in California's prisons. Some of the suits sought to reinforce state laws concerning the rights of mothers to be with their newborn babies, but more alleged that prisoners were being deprived of 'adequate prenatal and post partum medical care in violation of the constitutional prohibition against cruel and unusual punishments' (Barry, 1985). Such suits could not of course be brought here. England has no written constitution and the class action does not exist. But what many interested parties still find hard to believe is that there are *no* mechanisms in Britain whereby conditions in prisons can be challenged in the courts. This is because English prisons are protected by Crown Immunity from any criminal or civil proceeding being brought against them and, in any case, there is no code of minimum standards to which intending plaintiffs could refer. (See Casale, 1984 on minimum standards; and Stern, 1989:79–84 on Crown Immunity.) Within the prisons, too, there are no effective complaints procedures for inmates (see Maguire *et al.*, 1985), and prison administrators in England have often shown hostility to the whole concept of prisoner grievance machinery. As for the courts, as Vivien Stern points out,

The spirit of Lord Denning's famous comment, made in 1972, 'If the courts were to entertain actions from disgruntled prisoners, the governor's life would be made intolerable. The discipline of the prison would be undermined' lives on.

(Stern, 1989:83)

Yet deputies (jail staff) in the Californian women's jails argued that the use of grievance procedures could benefit staff as well as prisoners. First, instead of arguing with prisoners, they could refer them to the grievance procedure; second, in referring prisoners to the grievance machinery, they could indicate to them that the bad conditions were not of their (the staff's) making and that they too wished for them to be remedied. A deputy at the women's facility at Milpitas explained

Sometimes we say, 'You should "grieve" it' – either if we're tired of arguing with them or if we think something should be changed. Because it will be taken more seriously if *they* 'grieve' it than if *we* complained. Because *we* haven't any power.

But the history of the Prison Service in England and Wales has been one of a centralized and hierarchical penal estate *not* organized to allow the gaoled and their gaolers to work out an amicable mode of operation based on mutual respect. One might therefore suspect that part of the hostility of government both to the implementation of a code of minimum standards and the establishment of an effective grievance machinery is that each would not only increase the amount of control prisoners exercise over their treatment and living conditions, but also increase the power of prison officers *vis-à-vis* central government.

In addition to a legal *framework* for British prisons there is need for a legal *service*, and particularly for women prisoners. A majority of complaints from female ex-prisoners concerns the medical treatment they received (or failed to receive) in gaol, while a major source of anxiety for female inmates has usually centred around legal issues relating to child custody, divorce and landlord and tenant problems. Regular law clinics in women's prisons might serve the twin purposes of (1) ensuring that women have a legal advisor standing between them and the unchecked power of the Prison Medical Service, and (2) allowing them access to legal advice about, and representation in, any litigation touching upon their interests during the time they are serving sentence.

2 Establishment of a network of halfway houses for imprisoned addicts and their babies

An increasing proportion of hard drug misusers are women. We are particularly concerned at the number of young female addicts, some of whom are pregnant and have young children.

(Social Services Committee, 1985, quoted in Oppenheimer, 1989)

Section 3410 of the California Penal Code permits selected low-risk women with children under 6 years old to serve part of their sentence with their children in a residential setting instead of a prison. In 1987 I visited one such facility in San Francisco – the Elizabeth Fry Centre – where ten women prisoners and their children were living together in a large and well-appointed house in a good residential area. (I make the point about the area because so many offender-service agencies in the UK are located in substandard accommodation in the worst parts of a city.) Although the centre was run under prison regulations and inmates were regularly urine-tested for drugs, the women appeared to enjoy a degree of autonomy concerning the care of their children which is seldom achieved in prisons. Additionally, the centre offered child care to women who could find jobs, as well as employment training and counselling on substance abuse. Job workshops were also run. At the time of my visit in August 1987 only one woman had been returned to prison because of a positive urine-test.

In the third and final section of this chapter I shall be arguing that the numbers of women drug misusers in prison should be drastically decreased. However, women drug users who commit crime to fund their habits do need help. In view, therefore, of the extraordinarily poor rehabilitative facilities for female drug misusers, all gaoled women with a drug problem should be offered the opportunity to serve the last half of their sentences in an all-female drug rehabilitation community with the option of staying on in that community (in a part not governed by prison regulations) after their sentences have been completed. Such facilities should be open both to mothers and children and women without children.

3 Provision of visitors' centres at every prison

Although one of the pains of imprisonment frequently touched upon in the literature about incarceration is the pain caused by 'the visit' (see Cohen and Taylor, 1972; Boyle, 1977; Carlen, 1983a; Peckham, 1985; Save the Children Fund, 1989), almost nothing has been done to remedy the situation. (The Save the Children Fund has recently set up visitors' centres at three men's prisons.) The agony which imprisoned mothers suffer is seldom assuaged by a visit, and while in some cases the whole family dissolves in floods of tears, in other visits mothers watch with dismay as their young children ignore them and turn instead to their carers for attendance to all their needs. Adult visitors may bring other kinds of distressing news, for example, of the breakup of a relationship, the commencement of divorce or child custody proceedings, or impending eviction from the family home, etc. On occasions a woman may become distraught because her visitor arrives late or does not turn up at all. Whatever the cause of women inmates' visit-induced anxiety, the situation is not helped by the cramped and very public conditions wherein prisoners presently receive all kinds of devastating news without benefit of counselling facilities and prior to a post-visit strip-search and a return to cellular confinement. Recent proposals made by the Save the Children Fund (see below) would allow women in receipt of troubling news immediately to seek practical advice. Additionally, I would suggest that upset women should not be returned to their cells until they have been able to talk out the problem with (where appropriate) the relevant expert and/or a supportive listener.

Visitors' Centres should have a welcoming atmosphere, be attractively decorated and have good quality fittings and equipment.

The building should provide:

- toilets and baby changing facilities.
- a suitable play area.
- canteen facilities.
- a quiet room for those who need privacy.
- a room where confidential matters may be discussed.
- a comfortable waiting area.
- a public telephone.

The services provided should include:

- play matched to the needs of the children, available before and after a visit or when a parent wishes to see his/her partner alone.
- advice on child development and the management of behavioural problems, e.g. bedwetting, lying, stealing, attention seeking, aggression, withdrawal.
- inexpensive food and drinks.
- listening ears for those who need someone to talk to.
- specialist advice and information on benefits, welfare rights, housing, taxes, debt, legal representation, legal aid, court procedure and the criminal justice system.
- general information on health, education, prisons, transport, visiting procedures, prisoners' allowances (parcels), etc.
  (While some of the information is probably available in their own communities our work shows that extensive use is made of this service.)
- a system for linking families with sources of continuing support in their own communities, e.g. the Probation Service, Education and Welfare Officers, the Educational Psychology Service, Social Services, C.A.B., Parent and Toddler Groups, Family Centres, Churches and other community based voluntary organisations.

(Save the Children Fund, 1989)

A feminist jurisprudence

I am constantly asked whether I think it possible (and/or desirable) to develop a distinct and different way of thinking about female law-breakers and state punishment, whether in fact a feminist jurisprudence can or should inform the management of women's prisons, the writing of social inquiry reports for women, and the running of women offenders' hostels or probation groups, etc. The question is an important one. For as Carol Smart has recently observed,

> The search for a feminist jurisprudence signals the shift away from a concentration on law reform and 'adding women' into legal considerations to a concern with fundamental issues like legal logic, legal values, justice, neutrality and objectivity.
>
> (Smart, 1989:66)

Yet although Smart argues that we do indeed need to theorize women's oppression, she expresses reservations about the quest for a feminist jurisprudence. Among these reservations are fears: (1) that a feminist jurisprudence would merely replace one closed and global system of 'Truth' with another and that, consequently, application of some principles of a feminist jurisprudence (e.g. equality, the appeal to certain 'rights') might result merely in advancing certain feminist claims to the detriment of others; and (2) that 'the problem of attempting to construct a feminist jurisprudence is that it does not de-centre law' (ibid.). Certainly, too, Smart's own analyses in her book, *Feminism and the Power of Law*, elegantly and incisively illustrate that when women go to law in civil cases: they too often find that even when their claims are rooted in the apparent logic of legislative reforms which could be expected to right women's wrongs, 'once enacted, legislation is in the hands of individuals and agencies far removed from the values and politics of the women's movement' (Smart, 1989:160). But law avoidance is an option not open to women law-breakers who, of course, stand before the law not voluntarily seeking remedy but involuntarily awaiting punishment.

The question of what to do about women law-breakers has been a thorny one for feminists. It is one thing to search for a feminist jurisprudence . . . but who wants a feminist penology? Well, people involved in the criminal justice and penal systems might, for a start. Concerned women working in the courts, prisons and non-custodial agencies might find it helpful to have some general feminist guidelines on penal policy, while law-breaking women might find themselves to be less frequently written out of the judicial and penal scripts (Worrall, 1989) if a programme of criminal justice for women were to be among other (preferably socialist) paradigms informing the administration of criminal and penal justice for female law-breakers.

I take Carol Smart's point that 'jurisprudence' – a systematized knowledge or theory of law – 'implies a global set of principles', but, at the same time, I would argue that use of the indefinite article can put *any* jurisprudence in its place. For although I myself can conceive of the possibility of several feminist jurisprudences – i.e. perspectives on the interpretation of laws which are informed by knowledge of women's varied (but usually distinctly different to men's) experiences – I can also think of several other 'non-feminist' jurisprudential and political consider-ations which might rightly inform decision making and assessments by both judi-cial and para-legal experts in criminal cases involving women. For instance, and as we saw in Chapter 4 earlier, probation officers can sometimes correctly calculate that if they argue for equality of provision for their women clients, their claims will be answered by the withdrawal of the existing facilities in question from their male clients. Likewise, a competent feminist probation officer might know, on the one hand, that her client will gain advantage if it can be demonstrated that she is a good housewife and mother. On the other hand, by privileging that woman's house-wifely and mothering performances she will also be colluding in, and promoting, the stereotype of the criminal woman who is NOT a wife and mother, and thereby possibly disadvantaging single, divorced, childless and lesbian female offenders. That such dilemmas exist should not be surprising. The constellations of political, ideological and economic conditions in which penal philosophies are realized mean that we can seldom expect to read-off a penal policy from a jurisprudence – whether it be called feminist, marxist, liberal or whatever. This is Smart's point, too, and it is because she recognizes the limits to theory that she recommends feminists to adopt a deconstructionist approach to law, and constantly call into question its claims to 'Truth'. None the less, because of the 'involuntary' relation-ship between women law-breakers and the criminal law, and because, too, women have traditionally been so invisible in the criminal justice and penal systems, I do think that in relation to this (criminal) branch of law feminists might both engage in the deconstructionist struggle *and* suggest principled ways in which the criminal justice and penal systems might become more women-wise. And now, before spelling out what such guidelines might involve, I make a digression.

The need for a feminist jurisprudence and a women-wise penology – the case of the 1989 report

On 21 April 1989 the Chief Inspector of Prisons' Report on HM Prison and Young Offenders Institution Drake Hall was published (Home Office, 1989c). It is a sensitive and interesting report with comprehensive coverage of all aspects of prison life and makes over 100 recommendations to the Governor. My concern here, however, will be with just one of its revelations – the difficulty which prison administrators appear to have in conceptualizing women prisoners and women's prisons. The significance of this is at least threefold. First, it becomes apparent that masculinist culture is seen to be an essential element of a *real* prison. Second, bereft of the masculinist yardstick, the inspectors have no consistent criteria for assessing the regime's relevance to the women's needs. Third, once they have accepted that women prisoners' needs may be different to those of men, the Report's authors find it difficult to 'make sense' of either Drake Hall or its inmates; they both raise the question as to whether the majority of women there need to be in prison at all, *and* remind the Governor that, none the less, Drake Hall 'remains a prison and should be managed as such' (p. 33).

To begin with, the population of Drake Hall (an open prison) is seen to be contingent upon contemporary penal politics:

> There were women convicted of very minor offences including failure to pay fines who, in a slightly different sentencing atmosphere, might well expect not to be sent to prison. There were also a number of women from abroad who were convicted of drug related offences and faced deportation towards the end of their sentence. It may well be that in the future deportation will come earlier.
>
> (HM Inspectorate of Prisons,
> Information Release 21 April 1989)

How had the women been allocated to an open prison? The inspectors 'concluded that the allocation of women to open conditions still owes much to immediate expediency and little to any reasoned system' (p. 32). But a 'reasoned system' for allocation can hardly be expected of a prison system which has no consistent criteria for assessing either law-breaking women or the regimes to which they are subject. Certainly at the time of inspection (autumn 1988) the Governor did not see Drake Hall as a prison. Instead he preferred to conceive of it as an extended family. (With himself as Patriarch?) Or a boarding school. (With himself as Head-master?) The inspectors were critical of this blatantly patriarchal attitude and the passages in which they discuss it are worth quoting because they illustrate the difficulties attendant upon the concept of a 'caring (non-masculinist) prison'.

> 3.6. In his Annual Report for 1987/88 the Governor said: 'My role as Governor of this female establishment has been more akin to that of the head of a large extended family. This has demanded an intensely personal style of management.' In briefing us at the beginning of our inspection he suggested that Drake Hall was more like a girls' boarding school than a prison. Some of this was borne out by what we saw. Our view, however, is that whilst it is very commendable to develop and maintain in a prison the best of the caring relationships of an extended family and ethos of a good boarding school, it remains a prison and should be managed as such. There are also negative features of the extended family and it is by no means always an efficient form of organization. It was clear too that the majority of prisoners at Drake Hall did not want to be treated as if they were in a boarding school. That having been said, it was a small establishment with a strong network of pleasant informal relationships. Over the years it had developed a very caring ethos. . . .
>
> 3.7. The difficult task facing the Governor will be to create a more account-

able and efficient organization without, at the same time, losing the warmth
and informality which characterizes the establishment.

(pp. 33–4)

It is interesting that 'accountability' and 'efficiency' are seen as being antithetical to
'warmth' and 'caring' and to note that no male establishment is cited as being able
to combine these supposedly opposed qualities. Indeed, apart from suggesting that
inmate committees be formed (as in male prisons), the inspectors again and again
admit their inability to explain some of the already well-known features of
women's imprisonment. For example, why in a supposedly 'caring' environment
are there such disproportionately high rates of reported offences against discipline
(pp. 36–7)? Why is 'throughcare' more honoured in the breach than the observance (p. 47)? Are women prisoners really more 'dependent' than their male
counterparts? Or is this apparent 'dependency' a product of the closer supervision
on the 'house-family' units (pp. 86–7)? It is difficult to see how the Governor (or
anyone else) could develop a consistent administrative policy on the basis of the
contradictory answers given in response to these different questions. On reported
offences against discipline, the Report has this to say:

3.17. It seemed that the higher rates of reported offences probably related to
the higher staff-to-inmate ratios in open prisons for women. Drake Hall had
between two and three times as many officers per inmate as we would expect
to find in an open prison for men and, in 1986, there were nearly three times
as many reported offences against discipline as in open prisons for men. We
saw nothing to suggest the women inmates behaved more badly in open
prison than their male counterparts. On the contrary, they seemed if anything
more willing to conform. We concluded, therefore, that the relatively high
staff to inmate ratios not only increased the opportunities for women inmates
to commit offences of disobedience or disrespect but also increased the likelihood of their being reported. . . .

[However, in para. 3.18.] Given the atmosphere of Drake Hall as we found it
we were not surprised to find any report [sic] for disrespect or abusive behaviour in the sample of 50 [studied]. This was, we thought, one of the most
reliable indicators of the generally courteous relationships between staff and
inmates.

(p. 37)

On 'throughcare':

3.46. There was no evidence of a cohesive, structured throughcare plan
which challenged inmates about the nature of their offending and gave them
an opportunity to work out with staff how they might use the resources
available at Drake Hall to restructure their life style if they chose to do so. . . .

We felt that this reflected management's uncertainty about what it was trying to achieve during a woman's sentence. . . .

3.56. . . . We thought that in view of the constraints laid upon the Governor and the ACPO to produce a structured programme for the throughcare of young offenders under the terms of the new unified sentence, now might be an appropriate time to form new guidelines for the throughcare of all offenders at Drake Hall.

(pp. 47, 51)

And, most tellingly, on 'dependency' and 'house-family' units:

3.155. . . . Inmates' needs and willingness to express their problems were much greater than we would expect to find in male establishments. The staff (particularly but not exclusively on the houses) responded patiently and constructively. The inmates also seemed to care for and support each other to a considerable extent. We speculated that women in prison have a marked need for a network of supportive relationships of a *familiar* kind and that women officers respond *naturally* to this. We thought that the emphasis on developing a 'house family' atmosphere in the three houses was very commendable. However, as we said above, the extended family is not necessarily an efficient form of organization; it can also foster dependency rather than inter-dependency. [And later]

3.159. . . . Whilst we applaud the idea of developing the 'house family' atmosphere we detected an element of over-supervision here, too. There seemed to us to be considerable scope for . . . using inmate committees as a means of extending programmes.

(pp. 83–4, emphasis added)

The inspectors considered the

possibility that women officers felt a stronger need for closer supervision of their charges than their male counterparts. It could be argued too that their charges actually need more support and supervision. However, we felt that the inmates at Drake Hall might respond well to rather less supervision and more involvement in decisions about their day-to-day lives. . . .

[para. 4.5]

4.7. We appreciated that, for various reasons, women adapt far less readily to imprisonment than men tend to do. They may or may not have more problems and anxieties than their male counterparts but they expressed them much more readily than men would in similar circumstances. If Prison Officers are to take a primary role in supporting inmates and helping them to deal with their problems, including their offending (and we believe that they should) then the ratio of higher [sic] officers to inmates is justifiable. One corollary of this would be that imprisonment, as a sentence for women, must be a consid-

erably more expensive option than imprisonment for men and the Courts
should know this.

(pp. 86–7)

My purpose in quoting from the Report at length was not to critique it. Indeed the
Chief Inspector takes a commendable deconstructionist stance in several passages,
calling into question: current sentencing policy which imprisons so many minor
female offenders; the 'house-family' organization of living quarters; and the over-
supervision that appears to be one unacceptable face of 'caring' in prison. Similarly
commendable are the recommendations concerning the formation of various inmate committees which might lead to the more democratic control of, for instance, catering, leisure and some rule changes. Yet, at the end of it all, one is still
left with the stereotypes of 'women' who 'naturally' care and who have a greater
'need' than men for 'familiar' relationships, more support and *therefore* a higher staff
to prisoner ratio than their male counterparts! And maybe 'over-supervision' could
be turned into more positive support – *but not in a prison*. For the conclusions to the
Report commence with a reassertion that although the Inspectorate

> were impressed, for the most part, by the caring and considerate way in which
> inmates were treated. . . . Drake Hall is bound by the same policies and rules
> as the rest of the Prison Service. We found too many areas in which regula-
> tions and policies relating to inmates and staff had been ignored or set aside.

(p. 85: para. 4.1)

So much for the possibility of developing a women-wise institution! And *that* is
why I quote from the Report at length: throughout, its authors did seem to be
attempting to theorize the 'as-yet-untheorized' – the implications for penal policy
of the recognition that women's experiences are different to men's. This Report
more than any other official penal discourse in recent times demonstrates the need
for the development of a feminist jurisprudence *and* a women-wise penology. As
far as imprisonment is concerned, such perspectives would call into question not
only women's imprisonment but also men's (e.g. why shouldn't men's gaols be run
on 'caring' lines? If petty female offenders should not be gaoled, why not empty
both men's and women's prisons of minor offenders?). But those issues are dealt
with in more detail in this chapter's closing section. Before concluding by outlining a strategy for the abolition of women's imprisonment, let us briefly discuss
what form a women-wise penology might take in the meantime, and how it is
already influencing (or might in the future influence): the writing of social inquiry
reports for women; all-female hostels and housing schemes; and all-women law-
breakers' and ex-prisoners' self-support or agency-run groups.

A women-wise penology

Two fundamental aims of a women-wise penology might be to ensure:

1 That the penal regulation of female law-breakers does not increase their oppression *as women* still further.
2 That the penal regulation of law-breaking men does not brutalize them and make them even more violently or ideologically oppressive towards women in the future.

Three strategic principles informing policy might be:

1 *Remedial action* to redress the present wrongs of women in the criminal justice and penal systems.
2 *Resistance* to penal or other regulatory measures based on essentialized stereotypes of gender.
3 *Democratic exploration* of the many different possible modes of living in a variety of all-female (and, for women who want them, mixed) schemes and groups.

Already some people working with women law-breakers are utilizing both their knowledge of research findings and their experience of discriminatory practices and structures which disadvantage women to develop specific guidelines to resist and remedy such practices.

1 Social inquiry reports and sentencing

This is an area where concerned probation officers have already deployed innovative strategies. An extract from the Report to the Divisional Management Team of Birmingham North is an excellent example of a practical policy document informed by both research and professional experience.

> *Report to DMT of Birmingham North Working Party on Women's Issues strategy paper.*
>
> *The Role of the Court Duty Officer:* Reports are frequently requested, where there is no obvious need. Efforts should be made to intervene and forestall such requests with solicitors, court clerks and magistrates. Female offenders are automatically viewed as having problems, whereas male offenders are generally viewed in relation to the offence. Court Duty Officers should attempt to ensure women are dealt with similarly. Present attitudes ensure women shoot up the tariff system, and as a result reach custodial sentences at a much faster rate than men.
>
> *SIR Stage:* The issues outlined above must be borne in mind when preparing reports on women. Male offending is regarded as criminality: female offending as abnormality. Women single-handedly shoulder enormous burdens in relation to children, and the female offenders with which the Probation Service has contact, are overwhelmingly poor. This does not mean that they should necessarily be placed on Probation. There is evidence to suggest . . . that black women are even more likely to be placed on Probation than white

women, particularly for first offences, thus ensuring a rapid rise through the tariff.

In SIRs, comments relating to cleanliness of the home and levels of child care are frequently made, comments that are singularly lacking in reports on male offenders. Similarly, comments about children having different fathers are prejudicial to women and should not be detailed. Were such comments made in respect of male offenders (and generally they are not), they would not be judged in the same way. Awareness of language is therefore important, and forenames should not be used. The lack of formality (this applies similarly to male offenders) 'reduces' the defendant and does not accord them the respect we take for granted, for example, when preparing/or having prepared appraisal reports.

Community Service

Research indicates that Community Service has a 'male image', and whilst Community Service in Birmingham is seen as equally appropriate for women as for men, the fact that there are no female CS staff at . . . (apart from the Unit's Secretary) may reinforce consciously or unconsciously this image in the eyes of fieldwork colleagues. This needs to be considered in future when appointing staff.

Too often, POs are making recommendations for Probation without making referrals to CS. In our view, no woman should be excluded from consideration.

Regarding child care for clients' children, practice varies, from none at . . . to attempts at . . . to locate women in nurseries, where their children can accompany them. This is unsatisfactory practice, and merely mirrors female clients' experience in the home. Parents cannot properly perform under their Orders, when they are placed in situations where they continue to feel responsible for the care of their children.

Our proposals for action are therefore as follows:

* Court Duty Officers should intervene to prevent unnecessary requests for SIRs.
* POs should discuss in pairs their SIRs on women defendants, in order to avoid discriminatory attitudes and language.
* Copies of all SIRs on women defendants to be passed to SPO after typing for monitoring of language and eventual collation of results.
* No recommendations for Probation on first offenders to be made without discussion with SPO.
* CS to be *considered* in relation to all women defendants.
* Any difficulties regarding provision of child care for women defendants referred to CS to be brought to . . .
* A review to take place of the work performed by women under CSOs (a

necessary requirement under the new 'National Standards'). This information to be brought to the DMT.
* Divisional Policy Monitoring Committee to be asked to monitor and
  collate information from team SPOs regarding SIRs and disposals.

(Clare et al., 1988)

2 Accommodation schemes for women in trouble

As I said at the end of Chapter 3, until criminal justice policy is subordinated to,
and co-ordinated with, a strategy for social justice in general, we can expect
homeless and destitute recidivist offenders to continue to go to gaol. In the meantime, housing policy for women in trouble and ex-prisoners could be informed
(and often is) by women-wise strategies which would at least be supportive (rather
than destructive) of ex-offenders' attempts to fashion for themselves a satisfying but
non-criminal life-style. For example:

1 Places reserved for women in trouble whether in mixed or women-only hostels
  should be retained as such even if the result is occasional under-occupancy.
2 Except in the very few hostels where there is a preponderance of extremely
  disturbed or mentally incapacitated women, housing schemes and hostels should
  be run on democratic lines with all participants invited to be involved in decisions which affect their day-to-day living conditions.
3 The dependency/independency ideological couplet should be displaced by
  'move-on' and 'come-back' schemes which allow women to 'move back' in
  times of crisis and in any case regularly visit to partake of communal facilities
  (e.g. laundry) and collective activities.
4 Schemes should allow for as many different household forms and life-styles as
  possible, and for this reason even women in hostels should (ideally) have their
  own front door bells and front door keys.
5 Administrators of accommodation for mothers and children should not enact
  policies designed either to regulate female sexuality or to police parenting.

The Self-Help Organization for ex-prisoners (SHOP) in London is a good example of a housing scheme (bedsits, 'move-on' services and 'come-back' facility)
which allows women ex-prisoners their own space, combining a recognition of
their need for privacy and independence (own front door bell, own keys to room)
with support in terms of a weekly house meeting and provision of all cleaning
materials and servicing of kitchen machinery and utensils. Other women-wise
schemes are described in Chapter 3 – for example, Crowley House in Birmingham, Stockdale House in London and Longden House in Manchester.

3 All-women probation-run or ex-prisoner-run support groups

Chapter 4 revealed that many co-ordinators of all-women probation-run or other groups for women in trouble have already theorized their own and group members' reported experiences in order to fashion spaces where troubled women can remedy (by assertiveness sessions, legal rights information/action, and cooperative enterprise) some of the oppression they regularly suffer in their daily lives. Additionally, and most importantly, it was also generally recognized that the material and psychological conditions conducive of women's offending are often different to those conducive of men's. It is important that 'women-wise' probation groups continue to exist – and for the following reasons:

1 They provide a space for the remedy and resistance of women's oppression.
2 They provide a forum in which women can collectively, democratically and responsibly fashion principles for the future (self) governance of their lives.
3 Offence-focused groups, whilst recognizing that there is no essentially 'female' cause of women's law-breaking (only historically specific economic, political and ideological conditions), can slowly gain knowledge of the combinations of circumstances in which women most frequently choose to break the law and subsequently develop 'behaviour-changing' therapies which women recognize as being relevant to their needs.
4 The very existence (and popularity) of probation-run women's groups in neighbourhoods bereft of most other social amenities calls into question what the criminal justice system (CJS) and its agents are really for. And ensuing analysis demonstrates that far from being concerned primarily with serious law-breakers, the CJS and its officers are more frequently providing support services for people who might not have been in trouble at all if they had been in employment *and* in receipt of decent provision from the education, housing, health and welfare services.

I have not tried to draw up a blueprint for a 'women-wise' penology, but have merely outlined some guiding principles and existing good practice. Strategies must be flexible enough to meet changes in the economy, politics, ideology, law-breaking and law enforcement, and the main purpose of this book has been to show that despite constant government subversion of them, there *are* alternatives to women's imprisonment. Furthermore, I have argued that it is desirable that 'women-wise' penal strategies should be fashioned from overall policy calculations based at least in part upon a 'feminist jurisprudence'. I now end by outlining a strategy for the virtual abolition of women's imprisonment.

Women's imprisonment: a strategy for abolition

First, I shall argue that the present less-than-abolitionist approaches to effecting changes in women's imprisonment are unlikely even to reduce the female prison population. Subsequently I shall set out a strategy for the abolition of women's imprisonment, arguing that its implementation should be promoted as an experimental prototype for the gradual abolition of all imprisonment as we know it.

Most campaigning in relation to women's imprisonment has advocated reductionist programmes which have either separately, or in combination, emphasized
fundamentalist, pragmatist or rationalist approaches. I, personally, have a sympathy
with all three. The major criticism I have of them is that they do not work. And it
is worth examining *why* they have been so ineffective in achieving a reduction in
the numbers of women in prison.

The fundamentalist approach argues that reduction in the female prison population will be best (and most permanently) achieved by two fundamental changes
in society. First by reduction of the inequality, poverty and other types of social
deprivation which appear to characterize the lives of a majority of women in prison
(Mandaraka-Sheppard, 1986; Genders and Player, 1987). Second by a diminution
of the sexism and racism that result in the discriminatory sentencing which sends so
many poverty-stricken white, and even more black, women to gaol for relatively
minor crimes. This fundamentalist line of reasoning is one that I am fiercely
committed to myself (Carlen, 1988) and I believe that it should be developed and
forcefully put to future governments – some of which, I hope, will be more
sympathetic than the present one to collectivist approaches to crime control. Yet,
because the fundamentalist approach involves a political agenda which *cannot* be
put into operation by the present Government with its commitment to the com-
petitive individualism of a market economy, it cannot at the present time have
much effect on the size of the female prison population.

The pragmatist approach rests upon the following arguments: that the majority
of women in prison – i.e. fine defaulters, the mentally ill, persistent petty offenders,
drug importers and remand prisoners – should not be there at all (see Matthews,
1981); that viable alternatives to custody must be found; that with a drastic reduction in female prisoners, males could be drafted into the present female institutions;
and that in the ensuing 'mix nicks' all prisoners would share the benefits of a wider
range of facilities (see Seear and Player, 1986).

Apart from having strong doubts about the likelihood of co-ed jails benefiting
the majority of women inmates, I have a great deal of time for the pragmatist
position. Its major strength lies in its emphasis upon increasing public awareness of
the expense, waste and dangers of sending to prison women who, either because of
the petty nature of their crimes or because of the precariousness of their health,
could be better dealt with by non-custodial penalties. What it puts less stress upon
are the means by which such women are to be kept out of prison. By contrast,
rational reductionist programmes (though not rejecting the fundamentalist and
pragmatist approaches) focus primarily upon contemporary sentencing patterns
together with the myths and contradictions that sustain them.

The most persuasive and elegant expositions of the rational reductionist position
have been put forward by Andrew Rutherford in 1984, Louis Blom-Cooper in
1987 and 1988, and Andrew Ashworth in 1988. Their arguments are all slightly
different and all are directed at reduction of the whole prison population, not just
the women's. For Rutherford the rational approach would involve setting a target

of 50 per cent reduction in the prison population and then taking steps to limit and structure sentencing discretion so that the target might be achieved. Blom-Cooper puts greater emphasis upon establishing priorities of sentencing objectives, his own priorities being, first, crime reduction; second, victim support; third, denunciation; and fourth, *residual* imprisonment – 'to contain the few from whom society can be protected in no other way' (Blom-Cooper, 1988:48). Andrew Ashworth has for years promoted the notion of a Sentencing Council which would structure the discretion of the judges. (See Ashworth, 1989 for a most recent exposition.) These reductionist programmes are ones that, as far as they go, I totally support. So should the Government. The patent failure of imprisonment to reduce crime should in itself provide any cost-cutting and crime-conscious government with a major justification for reducing the prison population and keeping imprisonment as a residual punishment for criminals obviously too dangerous to be left at large. But, you might say, isn't that exactly what the Government itself was aiming at when it recently unveiled its ambitious plans for reducing both imprisonment and crime by bringing the pains of imprisonment into the community? Maybe it was. What I will argue is that despite the merit of the liberal reductionist programmes and regardless of the stated aims of the conservative reductionist programme of the present Government, there still remain major impediments to reduction which, although their removal is part of the reductionists' strategy, will continue to sabotage all reductionist programmes. These impediments will only be displaced by an abolitionist strategy. Before I explain *why* I think that, as far as abolitionism is concerned, women's imprisonment is the most suitable case for experimentation, let us look briefly at those aspects of the criminal justice system which are likely to continue to subvert the best attempts of liberals to reduce the numbers presently being given custodial sentences.

The major barriers to reducing the prison population at the present time inhere in three interrelated strands of sentencing logic which appear to be held so tenaciously that only an abolitionist strategy will force sentencers to abandon them. These three dominant tenets of contemporary sentencing logic are (1) that just as individuals are 'free to choose' whether or not to commit crime, they are equally 'free to choose' whether or not to complete a non-custodial sentence; in other words, sentence *feasibility* has not been a prime consideration of sentencers; (2) that 'tariff' sentencing provides the most penologically sound guide to sentencing recidivist offenders; and (3) that imprisonment must be the inevitable backup to all non-custodial orders. (The rational reductionists of course challenge this but until imprisonment is actually abolished as a punishment for non-compliance, it seems that sentencers will not address their minds to other measures.)

First of all, let's look at sentence feasibility and the tightening-up of non-custodial orders as recommended by the 1988 Green Paper, *Punishment, Custody and the Community*.

Although the traditional jurisprudential concern about the difficulties of assessing the impact of the same sentence on offenders in different circumstances continues to be discussed by leading writers on sentencing (e.g. Walker, 1980; Ashworth, 1983), this focus upon sentence *impact* has not been matched by a similar focus upon sentence *feasibility*. And there is a difference between the two. Whereas the principle of equality of impact raises questions about the possible inequality of pain or deprivation suffered by different offenders awarded the same punishment, the notion of sentence feasibility raises questions about the likelihood of extremely disadvantaged offenders being able successfully to complete *any* very demanding non-custodial order.

When *Punishment, Custody and the Community* was published in 1988 it was hailed by certain of the mass media as evidence of a new 'get tough' approach to offenders. This was primarily because of the Government's stated determination 'to increase the public's confidence in keeping offenders in the community by making all non-custodial orders subject to strict and punitive enforcement'. Yet in the cases of a majority of poverty-stricken female recidivist petty offenders, an over-punitive non-custodial order is just not *feasible*.

The problem of sentence feasibility and social circumstances comes about primarily in two ways. First, many people (and especially women) currently enduring domestic situations fractured by the pains of unemployment, low wages and poor housing are in no fit state to undergo further punishment in the community. Second, many areas of the country lack the communal facilities which provide for a decent standard of public life. Thus, while certain offenders might be perfectly willing to attempt compliance with specified non-custodial orders, their probation officers might rightly calculate that, given the tensions and frustrations already existing in their homes, their clients would be unlikely to complete any order involving constant home calls, curfews or house arrest. Similarly, in other cases, officers might know that while a lack of child-minding facilities would prevent some parents from doing community service, a dearth of public transport would equally prevent some clients from getting to and from suitable schemes. Additionally, it might also be unrealistic to expect emotionally and mentally damaged recidivist clients to complete a punitive, as opposed to a supportive, order. In a rational sentencing system, of course, sentencers would be obliged to accept a probation officer's assessment of the non-feasibility of a rigid non-custodial sentence in certain cases. And certainly in the cases of offenders bearing multiple social disadvantage, sentencers would attempt to do least harm by making non-punitive and totally supportive orders. Yet that is not what happens now and, given the punitive tone of the 1988 Green Paper, it is not what is going to happen in the future. Instead, the tightening-up of the non-custodial alternatives to prison is likely to result in sentencers imposing tougher alternatives regardless of the appropriateness or feasibility of the sentence, and in offenders then breaching the conditions of unrealistic orders and ending up in prison anyhow.

Thus, while sentencers are allowed greater independence than their collective wisdom most probably warrants, while they privilege the logic of the 'tariff' above the logic of sentence feasibility, and while they see prison as the inevitable backup to non-custodials, rational reductionist programmes are not going to work. To reduce the prison population we must first reduce the number of prisons; to reduce the number of prisons we must first abolish certain categories of imprisonment. Women's imprisonment is, for several reasons, a prime candidate for abolition. Those reasons can, first, be derived pragmatically from the characteristics of the female prison population and, then, be related more fundamentally to *possible* shifts in the social control of women and *desirable* shifts in the relationships between women and men.

In summarizing the data annually available in the prison statistics, Seear and Player (1986:4) concluded that

> there is little or no evidence to support the view that the women who are sent to prison have committed exceptionally serious crimes. In general their offences tend to be less serious than those of male prisoners; they serve relatively short sentences; they have fewer previous convictions and less experience of prison than men; and they tend to be reconvicted less frequently than their male counterparts.

At the other end of the scale, and looking at the types of offenders about whom the public might well be more concerned, on 30 June 1987 only 66 adult women and 8 young female offenders were serving life sentences, while just over 14 per cent (i.e. 165) of the adult female population under sentence had been convicted of violence against the person (Home Office, 1988b). Compare those 165 adult females with the 6,342 adult males (i.e. 22 per cent of the male sentenced population in prison on the same date who had also been convicted of violence against the person – ibid.), and it is, I think, reasonable to claim that the public might initially be more easily persuaded to experiment with the abolition of women's imprisonment than they would be with men's.

For on the grounds that imprisonment in general does NOT control crime, on the grounds that imprisonment in general is wasteful of resources, on the grounds that the only people who should be imprisoned are those whose crimes are so heinous that the rest of us need to be protected from them, and on the grounds that sentencers have NOT shown themselves to be amenable to gently persuasive attempts to curb their promiscuous use of imprisonment. *I am suggesting that, for an experimental period of 5 years, imprisonment should be abolished as a 'normal' punishment for women and that a maximum of only 100 custodial places should be retained for female offenders convicted or accused of abnormally serious crimes.*

Additionally, I am suggesting that during the 5 year period:

1 Women convicted or accused of abnormally serious crimes should only be imprisoned after their cases have been referred by the trial judge to a Sentencing Council who would make the final adjudication.
2 There would be close monitoring of the sentencing of all women and especially of those whose sentences ran counter to the usual 'tariff'.

3 A fundamental and far-reaching examination of *all* sentencing should be undertaken as called for by Andrew Ashworth (1988).

More fundamentally there would need to be a massive resourcing of accommodation and educational facilities for single women with children as well as an extensive network of hostels and independent but sheltered living units for young girls leaving Care and/or in trouble with their parents. Furthermore at a time when people are particularly worried about child abuse, it would be essential that the increasing numbers of households living in poverty receive help of a positive and supportive kind. A move towards a more community-oriented type of provision for families engaged in child-rearing and other types of care could immensely benefit mothers at risk of being child abusers.

At the moment, many of the women who land up in prison do so because they are living unconventional family lives. Keeping them out of prison by forcing them to live with a male in order to collect various welfare benefits or to get shelter for the night is retrogressive (see Carlen, 1988:161–2). Yet, despite previous bad experiences of 'family life', some women already in trouble with the law, and with a host of other problems stemming from poverty and a generalized feeling of marginalization, are, none the less, led by existing social policies to believe that their only way 'back in' again is via men or motherhood. All over the country there is a scarcity of women-only drug rehabilitation centres, women-only problem-drinking schemes, women-only education access schemes, ex-prisoner mother and child accommodation, etc. Yet instead of providing the required homes and decent jobs to the increasing numbers of poverty-stricken young women, we leave them to sleep rough, and to beg and to steal. Eventually we imprison them at an average net operating cost of £385 per individual per week (Home Office, 1988e), put their children into Care at an even higher cost – and then, after a few months, turn them out of gaol to begin the whole cycle again. And at a still spiralling cost in terms of crime and social waste! The abolition of women's imprisonment could provide the impetus for the development of a whole range of schemes to help women in trouble find their way again. And the average daily population of the women's prisons is still small enough – at 1800 – to make such a social experiment possible. BUT, you say, but . . . there are all the practical questions. For example:

1 What would happen to the women who presently go to prison?
2 What would happen to fine defaulters and women failing to comply with the conditions of other non-custodial orders?
3 What would happen to the staff of the women's prisons?
4 What about the women still going to prison? Can one really talk sensibly about the abolition of women's imprisonment while still countenancing custodial sentences for some women?
5 Finally, cynics might inquire, what would be done with the women's prisons? Would they merely be filled up by increasing numbers of male prisoners?

I will begin by considering my last question first.

1 What should be done with the women's prisons?

Years ago when I worked as a secondary school teacher for the London County Council (as it was then) caning was allowed in schools, and those of us who managed to maintain good order in our classes without resort to the stick often claimed that the only way to make the beaters find alternative and more effective modes of control was to take away their canes. That is what I now propose in relation to the women's prisons. Take away the women's prisons from the judges and the magistrates, deal with each abnormally serious crime as it comes along, and for the rest of the women work at feasible sentences combining denunciation of the crime with interventionary work on its causes (whether those causes be personal or social or both). As for the actual prison building . . . if (as we have been led to believe by the 1988 Green Paper) there really is the political will to reduce the overall numbers going to prison, then many good uses for the women's gaols could be found – without using them to increase the male prisoner population.

2 What should happen to the women who presently go to prison?

The proposal to abolish women's imprisonment (with the exception of 100-maximum-places to be retained for women convicted or accused of abnormally serious crimes, e.g. certain types of murder, violence or terrorism) does not constitute a greatly increased threat to public safety. The recent researches of Hilary Allen (1987a and b) indicate that already many women convicted of very serious crimes of violence are given non-custodial sentences. That being so, more could be done to increase public debate about the appropriateness of giving long gaol sentences to grossly damaged young women who may indeed have committed truly horrendous crimes against, say, their children but who certainly do not have their own problems addressed in prison. But these particularly unfortunate women constitute only a small minority of the female prison population. A much larger group is comprised of persistent petty criminals who are more of a nuisance than a threat, e.g. drug users who commit crimes to fund their habit, mentally and emotionally unstable women, and young women cut off by poverty and unemployment from parents and contemporaries in work. For all of these I would recommend supportive, non-punitive schemes designed, as I have already said, to be both denunciatory and rehabilitative. I would NOT recommend intensive schemes which would not be feasible. I WOULD recommend, for example, increased use of Community Service Orders combined with supportive probation-run women-only groups.

3 But what would happen to fine defaulters and women failing to comply with the conditions of other non-custodial orders?

A hallmark of the carceral society is that its members find it difficult to conceive of a penal system lacking imprisonment as the ultimate backup to every type of penalty. However, once imprisonment has been abolished as a back-up sanction, more positive penal ways and means would have to be found and, I suspect, much more care WOULD be taken to fix on a feasible sentence in the first place. Most probably a very small minority of offenders would stubbornly resist all attempts to regulate them. Unless they went on to commit very serious crimes we would just have to put up with their anti-social behaviour, do all that we could to fully compensate and/or protect their victims, pay decent wages and give full support to project workers involved with extremely difficult women, and NOT make things worse by slapping them into gaol in desperation.

Louis Blom-Cooper and others have also recommended that imprisonment cease to be used as a backup to non-custodials. However, the backup measures put forward by Blom-Cooper refer mainly to white collar criminals who COULD be made to suffer other deprivations. The majority of the poor, however, have little to lose but their freedom, and it is for this reason that imprisonment must be abolished – and not even used when all else fails. The price we pay for the scandal of poverty in this society is that we render the poor ineligible to pay their penal dues.

4 What would happen to the staff of the women's prisons?

Closing the women's prisons would mean that about 800 prison officers would need redeployment. There would be no need for the Home Office to sack them. With careful counselling and adequate retraining on full pay, those not choosing to take early retirement or redundancy payments could be found jobs in, for instance, debt counselling, administrative posts, and the courts, as court escorts and as assistants in some non-custodial schemes.

5 Finally, what can it mean to talk of the abolition of women's imprisonment at the same time as countenancing a continuance of custodial sentences for at least a very few women?

To me it refers to at least two processes: the transformation of penal custody for the relatively few women it is still found necessary to imprison; and the abolition of imprisonment for women as a 'normal' punishment available to sentencers.

With only 100 women (or less) in custody they could be kept in secure conditions which would give them independence and any help they needed (e.g. with addictions). Adequate payments could be made for relatives and friends to visit the unit from afar, and the relatively small numbers in the prison community could be offset by a large number of outside groups going in, and by adequate provision for family visits. Prison officers would be given a large role to play in the development of the unit and would be encouraged to share in all the educational and other facilities available to the prisoners.

With the abolition of women's imprisonment as a 'normal' punishment available to sentencers, other features of the criminal justice system might be called into question – for example the tariff system. Because the abolition of women's imprisonment would be relatively a small-scale 'abolition' as compared with men's, experimentation could be made during the 5 year period with both Sentencing and Sentencing Review Councils in relation to women offenders' cases; a variety of 'positive support', non-custodial orders could also be tried out – and with government funding. Every facet of the experiment would require monitoring.

Implementation of a women's imprisonment abolition experiment would not be cheap. On the contrary, in the short term its full and proper implementation would most likely cost as much as the present housing and maintenance of a female prison population of 1800. But with a female prison population reduced to 100 or less, the initial costs of community schemes involving accommodation and education projects could be met. Once the capital outlay had been made, community projects would be much cheaper to run than the labour intensive gaols.

But there is no VERY cheap way of paying for the problems caused by the positive links between crime, imprisonment and increasing inequality (Box, 1987). Unfortunately, excellent non-custodial projects are being run down or closed as a result of government policies. For example: in London the abolition of first the GLC and now ILEA has adversely affected the funding of campaigning and education projects for ex-prisoners; the operation of the Social Fund is preventing some rehabilitated prisoners from moving out of hostels into their own flats; it is expected that the operation of the Housing Act 1988 will diminish the housing available for ex-prisoners – and so on. It is this knowledge of the adverse effects present government policies are having on the best attempts of probation officers and others to keep women out of prison that makes me take the reductionist sentiments of the 1988 Green Paper, *Punishment, Custody and the Community*, with a pinch of salt. But something must be done. The choice is between continuing to squander millions of pounds on prisons or taking bold steps to stop legislators and sentencers seeing the prisons as being the ultimate panacea for all political, social and penal ills. Abolishing women's imprisonment for an experimental period might be one small step towards giving the criminal justice and penal systems the thorough shake-up they so desperately need.

Appendix
Agencies, projects and hostels visited

Probation services responding to the request for information on non-custodial projects and hostels for women

Avon
Berkshire
Buckinghamshire
Cambridgeshire
Cheshire
Cleveland
Cumbria
Derbyshire
Devon
Dorset
Durham
Essex
Gloucestershire
Hereford and Worcester
Hertfordshire
Humberside
Kent
Lancashire
Lincolnshire
Inner London

South East London
Manchester
Merseyside
Northumbria
Oxfordshire
Shropshire
Somerset
Staffordshire
Suffolk
West Sussex
West Midlands
Wiltshire
North Yorkshire
South Yorkshire
Dyfed
South Glamorgan
West Glamorgan
North Wales
Powys
Northern Ireland

Hostels and Accommodation projects visited

Birmingham

Crowley House (probation hostel for women, Selly Oak)

London

Delancey St Hostel (for women)
1 Greek St (for women)
59 Greek St (for women)
Inner London Aftercare and Resettlement Unit
Katherine Price-Hughes House (probation hostel for men and women)
Kelley House (bail hostel for women)
Self-Help Organization for Ex-Prisoners (Housing Association) Ltd
Stockdale House (hostel for women ex-offenders)

Manchester

Homeless Offenders Office (Greater Manchester Probation)
Longden House (for women)
Stopover Hostel (for women)
Turning Point (for relapsed alcoholics, male and female)
Women's Direct Access

Staffordshire

Elizabeth Trust (for women)
Highgate Hostel (for men and women)
Night Shelter (for men and women)
Staffordshire Probation Accommodation Officer (Hanley)

Probation-run women's groups providing information

West Midlands

Crowley House Day Centre (for women) – visit
Sandwell Activity Centre (for women and men) – visit
Smethwick Office Women's Group – visit

Cardiff

Westgate Office Women's Group – visit

Greater Manchester

Longsight Office Women's Group – visit
Wythenshawe Office Women's Group – visit

Staffordshire

Burton Women's Group (telephone interview with leader)
Kidsgrove Ladies Group (telephone interview with leader)
Rugeley Women's Group (telephone interview with leader)
Tamworth Women's Group (telephone interview with leader)

Miscellaneous projects visited

Clean Break, London
Community Service Office, Staffordshire Probation
Creative and Supportive Trust (CAST), London
North London Education Project
Rainbow Day Centre, Staffordshire Probation, Hanley
Women's Alcohol Centre, London
Women's Motor Mechanics Workshop Ltd, London
Women Prisoners' Resource Centre (NACRO), London
Women in Prison, London

Prisons providing information

Askham Grange (visit – information from Governor, prison officers, probation and education staff)
Bullwood Hall (visit – information from probation staff)
Cookham Wood (visit – information from probation staff)
Drake Hall (two visits – information from Governor, Assistant Governor, education and probation staff)
East Sutton Park (written information from probation)

References

Adler, Z. (1987). *Rape on Trial*. London, Routledge and Kegan Paul.

Alcock, P. (1989). 'A better partnership between state and individual provision: Social Security into the 1990s', *Journal of Law and Society*, 16(1), Spring.

Alcohol Recovery Project (1988). *Women's Alcohol Centre*. London, WRP.

Allen, H. (1987a). *Justice Unbalanced*. Milton Keynes, Open University Press.

Allen, H. (1987b). 'Rendering them harmless: the professional portrayal of women charged with serious crimes', in P. Carlen and A. Worrall (eds) *Gender, Crime and Justice*. Milton Keynes, Open University Press.

Allen, H. (1989). 'Sentencing women', in P. Carlen and D. Cook (eds) *Paying for Crime*. Milton Keynes, Open University Press.

Ashworth, A. (1983). *Sentencing and Penal Policy*. London, Weidenfeld and Nicolson.

Ashworth, A. (1988). 'The road to sentencing reform', in *Prison Reform*, No. 5. London, Prison Reform Trust.

Ashworth, A. (1989). *Custody Reconsidered*. London, Centre for Policy Studies.

Audit Commission (1986). *Managing the Crisis in Council Housing*. London, HMSO.

Auld, J., Dorn, N. and South, N. (1986). 'Irregular work, irregular pleasures: heroin in the 1980s', in J. Young and R. Matthews (eds) *Confronting Crime*. London, Sage.

Austerberry, H. and Watson, S. (1983). *Women on the Margins*. London, City University, Housing Research Group.

Banks, C. and Fairhead, S. (1976). *The Petty Short-Term Prisoner*. Chichester, Barry Rose.

Bardsley, B. (1987). *Flowers in Hell: An Investigation into Women in Crime*. London, Pandora.

Barrie, E. and Ross, J. (1987). *Offence Focussed Group for Women Offenders*. Manchester Probation Service, Wythenshawe Office.

Barry, E. (1985). 'Children of prisoners: punishing the innocent', *Youth Law News*, March–April, San Francisco, National Center for Youth Law.

Beaton, L. (1985). *Shifting Horizons*. London, Canary Press.

Benn, M. and Ryder-Tchaikovsky, C. (1983). 'Women behind bars', *New Statesman*, 9 December.

Berthould, R. and Casey, B. (1988). *The Cost of Care in Hostels*. London, Policy Studies Institute.

Bianchi, H. and Swaaningen, R. (eds) (1986). *Abolitionism: Towards a Non-repressive Approach to Crime*. Amsterdam, Free University Press.

Blom-Cooper, L. (1988). *The Penalty of Imprisonment*. London, Prison Reform Trust and Howard League for Penal Reform.

Box, S. (1987). *Recession, Crime and Punishment*. London, Macmillan.

Boyle, J. (1977). *A Sense of Freedom*, Edinburgh, Canongate.

Brittain, V. (1979). *Testament of Youth*. London, Fontana.

Brown, R. (1982). 'The education of women in prison', in W. Forster (ed.) *Prison Education in England and Wales*. London, National Institute of Adult Education.

Bull, D. and Wilding, P. (eds) (1983). *Thatcherism and the Poor*. London, Child Poverty Action Group.

Byrne, D. (1987). 'Rich and poor: the growing divide', in A. Walker and C. Walker (eds) *The Growing Divide: A Social Audit 1979–1987*. London, Child Poverty Action Group.

Cain, M. (ed.) (1989). *Growing Up Good: Policing the Behaviour of Girls in Europe*. London, Sage.

Campbell, B. (1984). *Wigan Pier Revisited: Poverty and Politics in the 80's*. London, Virago.

Carlen, P. (1976). *Magistrates' Justice*. Oxford, Martin Robertson.

Carlen, P. (1980). 'Radical criminology, penal politics and the rule of law', in P. Carlen and M. Collison (eds) *Radical Issues in Criminology*. Oxford, Martin Robertson.

Carlen, P. (1983a). *Women's Imprisonment*. London, Routledge and Kegan Paul.

Carlen, P. (1983b). 'On rights and powers: some notes on penal politics', in D. Garland and P. Young (eds) *The Power to Punish*. London, Heinemann.

Carlen, P. (1985). 'Law, psychiatry and women's imprisonment: a sociological view', *British Journal of Psychiatry*, 46, June 18–21.

Carlen, P. (1986). 'Psychiatry in prisons: promises, premises, practices and politics', in P. Miller and N. Rose (eds) *The Power of Psychiatry*. Cambridge, Polity Press.

Carlen, P. (1987). 'Out of care, into custody', in P. Carlen and A. Worrall (eds), *Gender, Crime and Justice*. Milton Keynes, Open University Press.

Carlen, P. (1988). *Women, Crime and Poverty*. Milton Keynes, Open University Press.

Carlen, P. (1989). 'Crime, inequality and sentencing' in P. Carlen and D. Cook (eds) *Paying for Crime*. Milton Keynes, Open University Press.

Carlen, P., Christina, D., Hicks, J., O'Dwyer, J. and Tchaikovsky, C. (1985). *Criminal Women*. Cambridge, Polity Press.

Carlen, P. and Cook, D. (eds) (1989). *Paying for Crime*. Milton Keynes, Open University Press.

Carlen, P. and Tchaikovsky, C. (1985) 'Women in prison', in P. Carlen *et al*. *Criminal Women*. Cambridge, Polity Press.

Carlen, P. and Worrall, A. (eds) (1987). *Gender, Crime and Justice*. Milton Keynes, Open University Press.

CAS (1985). *Co-ordinated Accommodation Scheme Report 1985*. London, NACRO.

Casale, S. (1984). *Minimum Standards for Prison Establishments*. London, NACRO.

Casale, S. (1989). *Women Inside*. London, Civil Liberties Trust.

Chambers, G. and Millar, A. (1987). 'Proving sexual assault: prosecuting the offender or persecuting the victim?' in P. Carlen and A. Worrall (eds) *Gender, Crime and Justice*. Milton Keynes, Open University Press.

Christina, D. and Carlen, P. (1985) 'Christina: in her own time', in P. Carlen *et al*. *Criminal Women*. Cambridge, Polity Press.

Clare, J., Byford, N., Gilbert, K. and Gill, M. (1988). *Report to DMT of Birmingham North Working Party on Women's Issues Strategy Paper*. September, West Midlands Probation Service, Perry Barr Office.

Clare, A. and Thompson, J. (1985). *Report on Visits Made to C1 Unit Holloway Prison*. London, National Council for Civil Liberties.

Coggan, G. and Walker, M. (1982). *Frightened for My Life*. London, Fontana.

Cohen, S. and Taylor, L. (1972). *Psychological Survival*. Harmondsworth, Penguin.

Conway, K. (ed.) (1988). *Prescription for Poor Health: The Crisis for Homeless Families*. London, London Food Commission, Maternity Alliance, SHAC and Shelter.

Cook, D. (1987). 'Women on welfare: in crime or injustice?', in P. Carlen and A. Worrall (eds) *Gender, Crime and Justice*. Milton Keynes, Open University Press.

Cook, D. (1989). *Rich Law, Poor Law: Different Responses to Tax and Social Security Fraud*. Milton Keynes, Open University Press.

Cresswell, J. (1987) in *CAST 1986–7 Report*. London, CAST.

Currie, E. (1985). *Confronting Crime: An American Challenge*. New York, Pantheon.

Day, N. (1989). 'For who's benefit?', *Probation Journal*, September.

Dobash, R., Dobash, R. and Gutteridge, S. (1986). *The Imprisonment of Women*. Oxford, Blackwell.

Dominelli, L. (1984). 'Differential justice: domestic labour, community service, and female offenders', *Probation Journal*, 3(3), 100–3.

Downes, D. (1988). *Contrasts in Tolerance: Penal Policy in the Netherlands and England and Wales*. Oxford, Oxford University Press.

Drake Hall Prison Education Dept. (1988). *Access Course*. Drake Hall (information sheet given to all prisoners).

Eaton, M. (1986). *Justice for Women: Family, Court and Social Control*. Milton Keynes, Open University Press.

Edwards, S.M. (1984). *Women on Trial*. Manchester, Manchester University Press.

Edwards, S.M. (1987). 'Prostitutes: victims of law, social policy and organised crime', in P. Carlen and A. Worrall (eds) *Gender, Crime and Justice*. Milton Keynes, Open University Press.

Farrington, D. and Morris, A. (1983a). 'Sex, sentencing and conviction', *Journal of Criminology*, 23(3), July, 229–48.

Farrington, D. and Morris, A. (1983b). 'Do magistrates discriminate against men?', *Justice of the Peace*. 17, September, 601–3.

Featherstone, B. (1987). *There Is an Alternative*. London, Prison Reform Trust.

Franklin, R.G. (1988). *The Demise of Council Housing: How Should the Probation Service Respond?* Paper presented at (Manchester) City Study Day, Friday 24 June.

Gamble, A. and Wells, C. (eds) (1989). 'Thatcher's Law', *Journal of Law and Society*, 16(1), Spring, special issue.

Genders, E. and Player, E. (1987). 'Women in prison: the treatment, the control, and the experience', in P. Carlen and A. Worrall (eds) *Gender, Crime and Justice*. Milton Keynes, Open University Press.

Genders, E. and Player, E. (1989). *Race Relations in Prisons*. Oxford, Oxford University Press.

Gibbens, T.C.N. (1971). 'Female Offenders', *British Journal of Hospital Medicine*, September.

GLC Women's Committee (1986). *Breaking the Silence*. London, Greater London Council.

Glendinning, C. (1987) 'Impoverishing women', in A. Walker and C. Walker (eds) *The Growing Divide: A Social Audit 1979–1987*. London, Child Poverty Action Group.

Glendinning, C. and Millar, J. (1988). *Women and Poverty in Britain*. Brighton, Wheatsheaf.

Gosling, J. (1988). *True Horror Stories*. London, Central London Social Security Advisers Forum (CLSSAF).

Graham, C. and Prosser, T. (eds) (1988). *Waiving the Rules: The Constitution under Thatcherism*. Milton Keynes, Open University Press.

Green, G., Firth, L. and Chandler, R. (1988). *Women's Housing Handbook*. London, Resource Information Centre.

Gropper, A. (1985). *Probing the Links between Drugs and Crime*. Washington, DC, US Dept. of Justice/National Institute of Justice.

Gunn, J., Robertson, G., Dell, S. and Way, C. (1978). *Psychiatric Aspects of Imprisonment*. London, Academic Press.

Hall, S. and Jacques, M. (eds) (1983). *The Politics of Thatcherism*. 'Introduction' by Editors, London, Lawrence and Wishart in association with *Marxism Today*.

Heidensohn, F. (1986). 'Models of justice: Portia or Persephone? Some thoughts on equality, fairness and gender in the field of criminal justice', *International Journal of the Sociology of Law*, 14(3/4), 287–98.

Hicks, J. and Carlen, P. (1985). 'Jenny: In a criminal business', in P. Carlen *et al. Criminal Women*. Cambridge, Polity Press.

Holborough, J. (1987) in *Clean Break 1986–7 Report*. London, Clean Break.

Home Office (1966). *Report of the Inquiry into Prison Escapes and Security by the Earl Mountbatten of Burma*. Cmnd. 3175, London, Home Office.

Home Office (1968). The Report of the Advisory Council on The Penal System, *The Regime for Long-term Prisoners in Conditions of Maximum Security*. London, Home Office.

Home Office (1973). *Education in Establishments for Women and Girls*. Policy Statement No. 5, Prison Department, London, Home Office.

Home Office (1981). *HM Prison Cookham Wood. Report by HM Chief Inspector of Prisons*. London, Home Office.

Home Office (1984a). *HM Borstal Bullwood Hall. Report by HM Chief Inspector of Prisons*. London, Home Office.

Home Office (1984b). *HM Remand Centre Pucklechurch. Report by HM Chief Inspector of Prisons*. London, Home Office.

Home Office (1985a). *Report of the Holloway Project Committee*. London, Home Office.

Home Office (1985b). *HM Prison Askham Grange. Report by HM Chief Inspector of Prisons*. London, Home Office.

Home Office (1985c). *HM Prison Holloway. Report by HM Chief Inspector of Prisons*. London, Home Office.

Home Office (1986). *The Ethnic Origins of Prisoners: The Prison Population on 30th June 1985 and Persons received July 1984–March 1985*. Home Office Statistical Bulletin 17/86, June 1986.

Home Office (1987). *HM Prison and Youth Custody Centre. East Sutton Park. Report by HM Chief Inspector of Prisons*. London, Home Office.

Home Office (1988a). *Criminal Statistics England and Wales, 1987*. Cm 498, London, HMSO.

Home Office (1988b). *Prison Statistics England and Wales, 1987*. Cm 547, London, HMSO.

Home Office (1988c). *Punishment, Custody and the Community*. Cm 424, London, HMSO.

Home Office (1988d). *HM Remand Centre Risley. Report by HM Chief Inspector of Prisons*. London, Home Office.

Home Office (1988e). *Report on the Work of the Prison Service April 1987–March 1988*. Cm 516, London, HMSO.

Home Office (1988f). *Circular No. 35/1988 Review of Non-Custodial Offender Accommodation*. London, Home Office.

Home Office (1988g). *Projections of the Long Term Trends in the Prison Population to 1996*. Home Office Statistical Bulletin 7/88, London, Home Office.

Home Office (1988h). *The Prison Population in 1987*. Home Office Statistical Bulletin, London, Home Office.

Home Office (1989a). *Projections of long term trends in the prison population to 1997*. Home Office Statistical Bulletin 11/89, 6 April, London, Home Office.

Home Office (1989b). *The Prison Population in 1988*. Home Office Statistical Bulletin 12/89, 6 April, London, Home Office.

Home Office (1989c). *Report of HM Chief Inspector of Prisons on HM Prison and Young Offenders Institution Drake Hall*. London, Home Office.

Hudson, B. (1987). *Justice through Punishment*. London, Macmillan.

Hunt, P. (1983). *Gender and Class Consciousness*. London, Macmillan.

HYPAC (1985). *The Work of Handsworth Young Persons Accommodation Committee*. London, NACRO.

Jones, H. (1983). *Moving On: A Guide to Independent Living*. London, NACRO.

Leach, S. and Stoker, G. (1988). 'The transformation of central–local government', in C. Graham and T. Prosser (eds) *Waiving the Rules: The Constitution under Thatcherism*. Milton Keynes, Open University Press.

Lester, A. and Taylor, P. (1989). *'H' Wing, HM Prison Durham*. London, Women in Prison.

McRobbie, A. and Garber, J. (1976). 'Girls and subcultures', in S. Hall and T. Jefferson (eds) *Resistance through Rituals*. London, Hutchinson.

McShane, Y. (1980). *Daughter of Evil*. London, WH Allen.

Maguire, M., Vagg, J. and Morgan, R. (eds) (1985). *Accountability and Prisons*. London, Tavistock.

Mair, G. (1988). *Probation Day Centres*. London, Home Office/HMSO.

Mandaraka-Sheppard, A. (1986). *The Dynamics of Aggression in Women's Prisons in England*. London, Gower.

Mathiesen, T. (1974). *The Politics of Abolition*. Oxford, Martin Robertson.

Matthews, J. (1981). *Women in the Penal System*. London, NACRO.

Mebarek, G. (1987) in *Clean Break 1986–7 Report*, London, Clean Break.

Mitra, C. (1983). Letter to *Community Care*, 23 September 1983.

Morris, T. (1988). 'Punishment, custody and the community', *Criminal Justice*, 6(4), London, Howard League.

NACRO (1981). *Bridging the Gap: The Report of a Working Party on the Transition from Education in Penal Establishments to Education in the Community*. London, NACRO.

NACRO (1982). *Supported Housing Projects for Single People*. London, NACRO.

NACRO (1985). *NACRO's Housing Services*. London, NACRO.

NACRO (1986a). *Black People and the Criminal Justice System*. London, NACRO.

NACRO (1986b). *They Don't Give You a Clue*. London, NACRO.

NACRO (1987a). *Women in Prison*. London, NACRO.

NACRO (1987b). *Women, Cautions and Sentencing*. London, NACRO.

NACRO (1987c). *Annual Report 1986–7*. London, NACRO.

NACRO (1987d). *Facing the Problem: A Report on Alternatives to Unemployment for Offenders*. London, NACRO.

NACRO (1988a). *Mothers and Babies in Prison*. Nacro Briefing, March, London, NACRO.

NACRO (1988b). *Annual Report 1987–8*. London, NACRO.

NACRO (1989a). *Women in Prison*. Nacro Briefing 33, London, NACRO.

NACRO (1989b). *Offences against Discipline in Women's Prisons*. March, London, NACRO.

NAPO (1988). *Probation Directory 1988*. Ilkley, Owen Wells for NAPO.

NAPO (1989). *Punishment, Custody and the Community: The Response of NAPO*. London, NAPO.

National Children's Home (1988). *The Children in Danger Factfile*. London, National Children's Home.

North London Education Project (1986). *Report 1984–86*. London, NLEP.

O'Dwyer, J. and Carlen, P. (1985). 'Surviving Holloway and other women's prisons', in P. Carlen *et al. Criminal Women*. Cambridge, Polity Press.

O'Dwyer, J., Wilson, J. and Carlen, P. (1987). 'Women's imprisonment in England, Wales and Scotland', in P. Carlen and A. Worrall (eds), *Gender, Crime and Justice*. Milton Keynes, Open University Press.

Oppenheimer, E. (1989). 'Young female drug users: towards an appropriate policy', in M. Cain (ed.) *Growing Up Good*. London, Sage.

Padell, U. and Stevenson, P. (1988). *Insiders*. London, Virago.

Pascall, G. (1986). *Social Policy: A Feminist Analysis*. London, Tavistock.

Pearson, G., Gilman, M. and Malver, S. (1986). *Young People and Heroin Use in the North of England: A Report to the Health Education Council*. London, Middlesex Polytechnic.

Peckham, A. (1985). *A Woman in Custody*. London, Fontana.

Prison Reform Trust (1985). *Prison Medicine*. London, Prison Reform Trust.

Raynor, P. (1988). *Punishment, Custody and the Community: A Comment on the Green Paper*. Swansea, University College.

Rosenbaum, M. (1981). *Women on Heroin*. New Brunswick, New Jersey, Rutgers University Press.

Rutherford, A. (1984). *Prisons and the Process of Justice: The Reductionist Challenge*. London, Heinemann.

Save the Children Fund (1989). *Prison Visitors' Centres: A Response to the Needs of Prisoners' Families*. London, Save the Children Fund.

Seear, N. and Player, E. (1986). *Women in the Penal System*. London, Howard League for Penal Reform.

Shaw, S. (1985). 'Introduction: the case for change in prison medicine' in *Prison Medicine*. London, Prison Reform Trust.

Shelter (1988). *Campaign Pack: Housing Bill*. London, Shelter.

Sim, J. (1981). *A Chance to Learn*. Manchester, NACRO.

Smart, C. (1989). *Feminism and the Power of Law*. London, Routledge.

Smith, A. (1962). *Women in Prison*. London, Stevens.

Smith, R. (1984). *Prison Health Care*. London, British Medical Association.

Social Services Committee (1985). *Misuse of Drugs with Special Reference to Treatment and Rehabilitation of Misusers of Hard Drugs (4th Report)*. London, HMSO.

Soley, C. (1986). 'Labour's Prison Policy', in *Politics and Prisons*. London, Prison Reform Trust.

Stang-Dahl, T. (1988). *Women's Law: An Introduction to Feminist Jurisprudence*. Oslo, Norwegian University Press.

Stern, V. (1989). *Imprisoned by our Prisons: What Needs To Be Done*. London, Unwin Hyman.

Stonham Housing Association (1988). *Annual Report 1988*. London, Stonham Housing Association.

Thomas-Crandon, J. (1988). 'Black female prisoners' scheme', *Criminal Justice*, 6 (3), London, Howard League.

Townsend, P., with Corrigan, P. and Kowarzik, V. (1987). *Poverty and Labour in London*. London, Low Pay Unit.

Train, C.J. (1988). 'Message from the Director General', *HM Prison Service Briefing*, 4, 14 November, London, Home Office.

United States Dept. of Justice (1987). *Prisoners in 1986*. Washington, DC, Bureau of Justice Statistics.

United States Dept. of Labor (1985). *The United Nations Decade for Women 1976–1985: Employment in the United States*. Washington, DC, United States Dept. of Labor.

Walker, H. (1985). 'Women's issues in probation practice', in H. Walker and B. Beaumont (eds) *Working with Offenders*. London, Macmillan.

Walker, N. (1980). *Punishment, Danger, Stigma*. Oxford, Blackwell.

Ward, T. (1988). 'Privatisation and Punishment', *Criminal Justice*, 6(4), London, Howard League.

Wheeler, P. *et al.* (1989). 'Persephone chained', *The Prison Journal*.

Wiles, P. (1988). 'Law, order and the state', in C. Graham and T. Prosser (eds) *Waiving the Rules: The Constitution under Thatcherism*. Milton Keynes, Open University Press.

Woolf, V. (1963). *A Room of One's Own*. First published by the Hogarth Press 1929, London, Grafton.

Worrall, A. (1981). 'Out of place: the female offender in court', *Probation Journal*, 28, 90–3.

Worrall, A. (1989). *Offending Women*. London, Sage.

WPRC (1986). *Annual Report 1985–6*. London, WPRC.

WPRC (1989a). Biennial Report 1st April 1987–31st March 1989. London, Women Prisoners' Resource Centre.

WPRC (1989b). *Reception Pack*. London, Women Prisoners' Resource Centre.

Yapp, A. (1987). *First Come, First Served? A Study of Emergency Night Shelters*. London, Resource Information Service.

Index